NONREQUIRED
READING

ALSO BY WISŁAWA SZYMBORSKA

Poems New and Collected 1957–1997

View with a Grain of Sand: Selected Poems

WISŁAWA SZYMBORSKA

NONREQUIRED READING

PROSE PIECES

TRANSLATED FROM THE POLISH
BY CLARE CAVANAGH

HARCOURT, INC.
NEW YORK   SAN DIEGO   LONDON

Requests for permission to make copies of any part of the work should be mailed to the following address: Permissions Department, Harcourt, Inc., 6277 Sea Harbor Drive, Orlando, Florida 32887-6777.

www.HarcourtBooks.com

Library of Congress Cataloging-in-Publication Data
Szymborska, Wisława.
[Prose works. English. Selections]
Nonrequired reading: prose pieces/Wisława Szymborska; translated from the Polish by Clare Cavanagh.—1st ed.
p. cm.
ISBN 0-15-100660-1
ISBN 979-0-1510-0660-1

1. Szymborska, Wisława—Translations into English.
I. Cavanagh, Clare. II. Title.
PG7178.Z9 A222 2002
028.1—dc21   2002002440

Designed by Linda Lockowitz
Text set in New Baskerville
Printed in the United States of America
First edition
A C E G I K J H F D B

Contents

❧

FROM THE AUTHOR

ঞ৷৹

I GOT THE IDEA OF writing *Nonrequired Reading* from the section called "Books Received" you find in many literary journals. It was easy to see that only a tiny percentage of the books listed later made their way to the reviewer's desk. Belles lettres and the most recent political commentary always received privileged treatment. Memoirs and reprints of the classics stood some chance of being reviewed. The odds for monographs, anthologies, and lexicons were much slimmer, though, and popular science and how-to books were virtually guaranteed to go unnoticed. But things looked different in the bookstores. Most (if not all) of the rapturously reviewed books lay gathering dust on the shelves for months before being sent off to be pulped, whereas all the many others, unappreciated, undiscussed, unrecommended, were selling out on the spot. I felt the need to give them a little attention. At first I thought I'd be writing real reviews, that is, in each case I'd describe the nature of the book at hand, place it in some larger context, then give the reader to understand that it was better than some and worse than others. But I soon realized that I couldn't write reviews and didn't even want to. That basically I am and wish to remain a reader, an amateur, and a fan, unburdened by the weight of ceaseless evaluation. Sometimes the book itself is my main subject; at other times it's just a pretext for spinning out various loose associations. Anyone who calls these pieces sketches will be correct. Anyone insisting on "reviews" will incur my displeasure.

One more comment from the heart: I'm old-fashioned and think that reading books is the most glorious pastime that humankind has yet devised. Homo Ludens dances, sings, produces meaningful gestures, strikes poses, dresses up, revels, and performs elaborate rituals. I don't wish to diminish the significance of these distractions—without them human life would pass in unimaginable monotony and, possibly, dispersion and defeat. But these are group activities, above which drifts a more or less perceptible whiff of collective gymnastics. Homo Ludens with a book is free. At least as free as he's capable of being. He himself makes up the rules of the game, which are subject only to his own curiosity. He's permitted to read intelligent books, from which he will benefit, as well as stupid ones, from which he may also learn something. He can stop before finishing one book, if he wishes, while starting another at the end and working his way back to the beginning. He may laugh in the wrong places or stop short at words that he'll keep for a lifetime. And, finally, he's free—and no other hobby can promise this—to eavesdrop on Montaigne's arguments or take a quick dip in the Mesozoic.

NONREQUIRED
READING

ABSENT-MINDED PROFESSORS

༄

A NECDOTES ABOUT GREAT people make for bracing reading. All right, the reader thinks, so I didn't discover chloroform, but I wasn't the worst student in my class, as Liebig was. Of course I wasn't the first to find salvarsan, but at least I'm not as scatterbrained as Ehrlich, who wrote letters to himself. Mendeleev may be light-years ahead of me as far as the elements go, but I'm far more restrained and better groomed regarding hair. And did I ever forget to show up at my own wedding like Pasteur? Or lock the sugar bowl up to keep my wife out, like Laplace? By comparison with such scientists, we do indeed feel slightly more reasonable, better bred, and perhaps even higher-minded as regards daily living. Moreover, from our vantage point, we know which scientist was right and which was shamefully mistaken. How innocuous someone like Pettenhoffer, for example, seems to us today! Pettenhoffer was a doctor who ferociously battled the findings on bacteria's pathogenetic powers. When Koch discovered the comma bacillus of cholera, Pettenhoffer publicly swallowed a whole testtubeful of these unpleasant microbes in order to demonstrate that the bacteriologists, with Koch at their helm, were dangerous mythomaniacs. This anecdote gains particular luster from the fact that nothing happened to Pettenhoffer. He kept his health and scornfully flaunted his triumph until the end of his days. Why he wasn't infected remains a mystery for medicine. But not for psychology. From time to time people do appear who have a particularly strong resistance to obvious facts. Oh, how pleasant and honorable not to be a Pettenhoffer!

Scientists in Anecdotes by Waclaw Golebowiez, second edition, Warsaw: Wiedza Powszechna, 1968.

The Importance of Being Scared

❧

A CERTAIN WRITER WITH a fairly vivid imagination was asked to write something for children. "Terrific," he exclaimed. "I've got an idea for something with a witch." The ladies at the publishing house threw up their hands: "Anything but witches; you musn't scare the children!" "What about the toys in the stores," the writer asked, "those walleyed teddy bears with magenta fur?" I personally approach this from yet another angle. Children like being frightened by fairy tales. They have an inborn need to experience powerful emotions. Andersen scared children, but I'm certain that none of them held it against him, not even after they grew up. His marvelous tales abound in indubitably supernatural beings, not to mention talking animals and loquacious buckets. Not everyone in this brotherhood is harmless and well-disposed. The character who turns up most often is death, an implacable individual who steals unexpectedly into the very heart of happiness and carries off the best, the most beloved. Andersen took children seriously. He speaks to them not only about life's joyous

adventures, but about its woes, its miseries, its often unde-
served defeats. His fairy tales, peopled with fantastic creatures, are more realistic than whole tons of today's stories for
children, which fret about verisimilitude and avoid wonders
like the plague. Andersen had the courage to write stories
with unhappy endings. He didn't believe that you should try
to be good because it pays (as today's moral tales insistently
advertise, though it doesn't necessarily turn out that way in
real life), but because evil stems from intellectual and emotional stuntedness and is the one form of poverty that should
be shunned. And it's funny, it's just plain funny! Andersen
wouldn't be a great writer without the humor that comes in
every shade from good-natured laughter to open mockery.
But I don't think he'd be the great moralist he is if he were
just kindness personified. He wasn't. He had his whims and
weaknesses, and in daily life he was insufferable. It's said that
Dickens first blessed the day that Andersen came to visit him
and settled into a little room full of welcoming bouquets. But
the second day he blessed was the one that took his guest
back into Copenhagen's fog. It would seem that two writers
who shared so many traits should have looked each other in
the eye until the day they died. Well, so it goes.

Fifth edition (just imagine!) of Hans Christian Andersen's *Fairy Tales*,
translated into Polish by Stefania Beylin and Jaroslaw Iwaszkiewicz,
Warsaw: Panstwowy Instytut Wydawniczy, 1969.

Shortchanged

ぴ

How many species of animals manifest their readiness for independent life almost immediately after birth! This thanks only to a nervous system the likes of which we can scarcely imagine and innate abilities that we, in our assigned domain, acquire only through years of hard labor! Nature deprived us of a thousand fabulous features. It's true that she gave us our intellect in exchange, but she apparently forgot that this would be our chief means of getting by in the world. If she'd kept that in mind, she would have transferred a great deal of basic information into the realm of heredity. It would have been only fair if we'd been born with the multiplication tables already implanted in our brains, if we came out speaking at least the language of our parents, ready to dash off a respectable sonnet or ad-lib a decent keynote speech. Every infant would thus get a running start into the lofty realms of speculative thought. In the third year of life he'd be turning out better essays than I do, and by the age of seven he would be the author of *Instinct or Experience*. I know that airing my grievances in the columns of *Literary Life* won't help matters, but I'm miffed. Droscher vividly describes the astonishing achievements of the nerve tissue that permits animals to see without eyes, hear through their skin, and scent danger without the slightest breeze. And all this is part of the opulent ritual of instinctual activities....Every instinct strikes me as worthy of envy, but one most of all: it's called the instinct for withholding blows. Animals often fight within the bounds of their own species, but their battles as a rule end bloodlessly. At a given moment one opponent backs down, and that's the end of it. Dogs don't devour one another, birds don't peck other birds to pieces, antelopes don't impale their fellow antelopes. Not because they're intrinsically sweet-natured. It's merely the work of the mechanism that limits the force of the blow or the compression of the jaws. This instinct vanishes only in captivity; and it frequently fails to develop among breeds cultivated artificially. Which comes to the same thing.

Instinct or Experience by Vitus B. Droscher, translated from the German by Krystyna Kowalska, Warsaw: Wiedza Powszechna, 1969.

BY THE NUMBERS

ઝ૪

MY FIRST ENCOUNTER with statistics occurred when I was eight or nine and my class took a field trip to an exhibit on alcohol. It was full of graphs and figures, which I of course no longer remember. But I vividly recall a brightly colored plaster model of an alcoholic's liver. We all crowded around this liver. We were even more captivated, though, by a chart on which a little red bulb lighted up every two minutes. The legend explained that every two minutes someone somewhere in the world died from alcohol-related causes. We stood enthralled. One girl who already had a genuine wristwatch methodically checked the light's accuracy. But Zosia W. had an even better reaction. She made the sign of the cross and started reciting *requiescat in pace*. Statistics has never provoked such immediate emotions in me since. A friend of mine finds a grand panorama of life in every statistics yearbook that he reads; he sees and hears the numbers, he even experiences olfactory sensations. I envy him. How many times have I tried to translate the figures into concrete images; one whole man appears before my eyes, then a woman plus a few tenths springs up beside him. This unusual couple proceeds to yield (approximately!?) two children who immediately start downing hard liquor, and by the year's end they've consumed four and a half liters. The picture is then supplemented by phenomena as terrible existentially as they are linguistically: the grandmother's morbidity and the grandfather's mortality. Irena Landau probably wrote *The Statistical Pole* for people with equally misguided imaginations. In her little book she tries to present a normal family in various real-life situations. Unfortunately, the Kowalski family feels statistically typical, which immediately turns them into abstractions, since no individual ever feels typical. The book is easily digestible, but not particularly nourishing. Large numbers are tamed only with difficulty, and rarely find a place in unforced conversation. In the end the author herself humorously advises the readers to pick up a statistical yearbook instead, since they're so hard to put down.

The Statistical Pole by Irena Landau, Warsaw: Iskra, 1969.

DREAM ON

ℐℐ

W<small>E DREAM, BUT SO</small> carelessly, so imprecisely! "I want to be a bird," this or that person will say. But if an obliging fate changed him into a turkey, he'd feel betrayed. That's not what he had in mind, after all. Still worse dangers are hitched to the vehicle of time. "I'd like to wake up in eighteenth-century Warsaw," you might think lightheartedly, imagining that that will do the trick. That naturally you won't end up anywhere but in the salons of His Majesty Stanislaw Poniatowski, who will take you by the arm with a kindly smile and escort you to the dining room for one of his famous Thursday Dinners. Meanwhile you'd actually blunder into the nearest puddle. As soon as you'd scrambled out, a carriage drawn by eight horses would enter the narrow street and plaster you, terrified, against the wall, then cover you from head to foot with mud again. And it's so dark you can't see your own nose, you don't know which way to go, you stumble through the backyards of various palaces in a chaos of unpaved lanes, heaps of refuse, and ramshackle hovels. Soon some ruffians come looming from the dark and seize you by your windbreaker. I'm not writing a novel, so I don't have to think up a way to rescue you from this predicament. It's enough that you're now seated in a tavern where they serve you a roast, but on a dirty plate. At your request, the innkeeper pulls his shirttail from his pantaloons and polishes the plate until it shines. When you express your indignation, he says that you must have been brought up in the backwoods if you don't know that that's how Prince Radziwill himself attends to his ladies. In the hotel, not having managed to persuade them to give you some water for washing, you throw yourself upon your mattress and the bedbugs throw themselves upon you. You finally fall asleep near dawn, but you're soon awakened by screams, because someone on the second floor has started a fire. Without waiting for the firemen, who haven't yet been invented, you jump out the window and, thanks only to the piles of stinking garbage in the yard, you break not your neck, but your leg. A novice barber sets your leg without an anesthetic. You can thank your lucky stars if you don't get gangrene and the bones grow straight. Limping slightly, you return to your own epoch and buy the book you should have started with: *Daily Life in Enlightenment Warsaw.* It will enable you to recover the proper balance between the prose and the poetry of those times.

Daily Life in Enlightenment Warsaw by Anna Bardecka and Irena Turnou, Warsaw: Panstwowy Instytut Wydawniczy, 1969.

MUSICAL CHAIRS

♪♫

U NFORTUNATELY, I CAN'T go into more detail about *Il trovatore*, even though I've sung it many times, since I'm still not exactly sure what it's about...." The famous Viennese tenor Leo Slezak makes this confession in his memoirs. And oh, what a heavy stone has fallen from my heart! So it's not just me, out there in the audience, who can't always figure out who's singing against whom, why the man who for some reason is dressed up as a servant suddenly turns out to be a ruddy, buxom maiden, and why this unusually well-nourished maiden should faint at the sight of another, considerably older maiden while calling her her darling, dearest long-lost little daughter. So it's not just me—the people up on stage don't know what's going on either! It turns out that opera guides like this one are required on both sides of the footlights. I don't need to advertise this book; the first edition vanished like water in the sand. I'll say only that it covers two hundred operas from Monteverdi to the 1960s. Each composer gets a brief biography, followed by a detailed summary of the opera's plot, and finally a quick discussion of its music.

I can't say that I got through all two hundred operas in one sitting. But I did read all the lists of characters with their vocal types. A strict personal politics prevails in the world of opera. Family relationships are prescribed by codes as inviolable as those governing primitive tribes. A soprano must be a bass's daughter, a baritone's wife, and a tenor's lover. A tenor may neither generate an alto nor copulate with a contralto. A baritone lover is a rarity, and it's best if he just settles for a mezzo. And mezzo-sopranos, in turn, should watch out for tenors— fate casts them most often as "the other woman" or in the even sorrier role of the soprano's best friend. The one bearded woman in the history of opera (see Stravinsky's *A Rake's Progress*) is a mezzo-soprano and naturally knows no happiness. Apart from fathers, basses ordinarily play cardinals, the powers of darkness, prison functionaries, and, in one case, the director of an insane asylum. No conclusion follows from these comments. I admire opera, which is not real life, and I admire life, which is at times a true opera.

The Opera Handbook by Jozef Kanski, second edition, Krakow: Polskie Wydawnictwo Muzyczne, 1968.

COMPULSORY HAPPINESS

✧

A LITTLE BIRD SITS in the tree / And wonders at human-ity, / Even the wisest man around / Can't tell where hap-piness is found." Still you're better off not knowing like a human than knowing like a bird. Birds are lunatics with no clue as to their own lunacy. Instinct, which orders them to fly off every fall and resettle somewhere else that may be tens of thousands of miles away, only appears to be kindly and con-cerned with their well-being. If all that mattered were better food supplies in a more temperate climate, more than one species would end its protracted flight far sooner. But these demented creatures fly on, over mountains, where unex-pected storms may smash them into cliffs, over seas, in which they may drown. Nature's goal is not even ruthless selection: there are circumstances that destroy both strong and weak alike. A vile fate plagues the wild goose near Lake Czana. It feels the impulse to take off while it's still molting and can't leave the ground. So it sets off southward on foot. This mass exodus is anxiously awaited by various birds of prey, alongside a mammal with a stick, i.e., man. The massacre begins—and though it's repeated regularly, year after year, century after century, not a trace of it remains in the species' memory. Nature plays an even more diabolic trick on the lemming, a gentle creature dwelling in burrows. Every so often these burrows get overcrowded, so the lemmings abandon their longtime homes en masse. To start another colony nearby? Not a chance—they start walking, just walking, for such is their hormonal destiny. They keep walking until they reach the sea, in which they drown. This species continues only thanks to those few individuals who remain at home in the old burrows. Human history holds similar episodes. Except that we aren't compelled to rejoice about all of this, while I suspect that animals, on top of everything else, are burdened with compulsory happiness. Blond wrote his book for young people. It comprises five stories: lemmings, wild geese, seals, elephants, and bison. With an eye to his young reader, Blond has fictionalized things slightly, but it's done in moderation and without baby talk. Thus adults may also read this book with profit and horror.

The Enigmatic Lemming by Georges Blond, translated from the French by Janina Karczmarewicz-Fedorowska, Warsaw: Nasza Ksiegarnia, 1969.

THE COST OF CHIVALRY

ᏨᎵᎮ

THE CID REALLY DID exist, and his wife really was a young woman by the name of Jimena. The Cid's bravery is likewise not in question. However, the legend exaggerates his implacable hatred of the Spanish Moors. At times he sided with the Moors against the Christians. The nickname "El Cid" comes from the Arabic Sidi ("my lord") and indicates the hero's familiarity with the Islamic world. But this is forgotten in the folk epic, which sets his life on a single fixed course: with the Spanish king against the Moors. The first songs about the Cid most likely arose a half-century after his death, that is, in the middle of the twelfth century. The version we have today dates from the thirteenth century. It's unlikely that it is the work of a single author; there were probably two writers, whom a copyist later turned into one person. Two separate tales are at work within the epic; one involves the Cid's feats of valor, while the second deals with family matters. Swords clash in the first part, whereas in the second you catch courtiers' whispers and the rustling of ladies' gowns. A naive sobriety and simplicity permeates both stories, but somehow

I prefer the first. It was written by a medieval Balzac. Soldiering is chiefly a financial undertaking in his eyes. You need gold in order to do battle, and you need to do battle in order to get gold. Since war is costly, it has also got to turn a profit. You've got to bank on future plunder, exact tributes, and—if you can swing it—swindle when borrowing money. A knight's head, before being shattered, was preoccupied with financial matters. The author never forgets the spoils of war for a minute; he reckons them with gusto and delight. We're still far removed from a consciously idealized chivalry. The poem reeks of an authenticity that has been slightly sanitized by the scent of absolute virtue when we get to the *Song of Roland*, for example. Anna Ludwika Czerny's translation is absolutely splendid. It keeps the complete internal freedom of this early epic. It conveys the peculiar medieval artlessness that strikes us as slightly perverse today.

Poema del Cid, translated from the Spanish by Anna Ludwika Czerny, afterword by Zygmunt Czerny, graphics by Jozef Wilkon, Krakow: Wydawnictwo Literackie, 1970.

SEEING THE LIGHT

♫

IT'S USELESS TO try to describe Vermeer's paintings in words. They'd be far better served by a quartet consisting of two violins, bassoon, and harp. But art historians must make do with words, for such is their vocation and profession. Kuno Mittlestadt has found a relatively easy way out: he places Vermeer's art against the backdrop of his age and sees the master himself as his era's proxy. Unfortunately, artists are never perfect spokesmen for their age—and from this angle Vermeer turns out to be the bard of a very narrow, private slice of reality. Does this fact diminish his work's greatness? Of course not; greatness derives at times from something different. Mittlestadt realizes this and thus seeks in the Dutchman's art elements of social criticism and signs of revolt against the flourishing middle class. And if these aren't evident in every painting, he works to see what isn't there. Thus in the famous *The Artist in His Studio* he perceives an ironic contract between the artist's "kitchen" and the model clad in muse's garb. The model's "artificial" pose is meant to be an "unmasking device" vis-à-vis the proclivities of a bourgeoisie already enamored of allegories and idealized views of life. It seems like a reasonable argument as long as we don't look at the picture. The model who's supposed to be doing the unmasking is a young girl wrapped in a ravishing azure robe, with modestly downcast eyes. She's posed, of course, but in a completely unforced, unpretentious way. If there's irony here, it doesn't emerge from the compositional contrast. It permeates the entire painting; it's present in the horn's gleam, the curtain's folds, and the light falling from the window onto the black-and-white marble floor. Moreover, we find this irony displayed with the same prodigality throughout the master's paintings. I was equally surprised by Mittlestadt's views on one of Vermeer's final canvases (the artist died young, at the age of forty-three). I have in mind the *A Lady Standing at the Virginal.* According to this critic, the work signals both the age's decline and the waning of the artist's inspiration: it is cold, artificial, and calculated. The lady standing by her instrument is, he writes, psychologically "isolated" in her "monumentally frozen gesture." I look and disagree at every turn. I see a miracle of daylight falling on different materials: human skin, the silk gown, the chair's upholstery, the whitewashed wall. Vermeer constantly repeats this miracle, but in fresh variants and dazzling new permutations. What on earth have coldness and isolation got to do with this? The woman puts her hand on the virginal as if she'd like to play us a passage in jest, to remind us of something. She turns her head toward us with a lovely half-smile on her not particularly pretty face. The smile is thoughtful, with a touch of maternal forbearance. And for three hundred years she's been looking this way at all of us, including critics.

Jan Vermeer van Delft, compiled and with commentary by Kuno Mittlestadt, translated from the German by Anna M. Linke, eleven color and five black-and-white plates, Warsaw: Arkada, 1970.

THAT'S THE SPIRIT

♪

A STROLOGY, ALCHEMY, fortune-telling, black and white magic, numerology, chiromancy, necromancy, phrenology, theosophy, occultism, spiritism, telepathy: the authors have tossed all these things in the same sack and given them all a good thrashing. Each topic receives roughly the same mix of pity and disdain. I personally would prefer a certain hierarchy, since not all fads are created equal. The social consequences of devil-worship were different from those produced by the amiable search for the philosopher's stone, and one doubts the existence of brownies more energetically than one does the reality of telepathic phenomena. The book is at its best in depicting the historical and cultural background of such beliefs, and in its portraits of prominent magi, prophets, and founders of various sects. The authors have picked particularly extreme cases, in which fanaticism joins forces with skulduggery. A parade of incredibly eccentric personalities passes before our eyes—eccentrics as dreamed up by a gifted surrealist. But don't let anyone think for a minute that conjuring charms was a bed of roses, an easy way to earn one's daily bread. Such types generally led a nomadic, precarious existence: no rest, constant stress, caution, vigilance, the on-going need to create an uncanny impression. The ceaseless composing of letters, manifestos, sensational confessions—and this in the name of spirits who were often reluctant to co-operate. For charms you required secret contraptions and elaborate productions. At any moment your equipment might give out, your confederates might betray you, your followers might abandon you en masse for the competitor's camp. The alchemist Sedziwoj once married another al-chemist's elderly widow because he suspected (mistakenly, as it turned out) that she had access to her deceased spouse's se-crets. The theosophist Madame Blavatsky, a lady weighing in at well over two hundred pounds, was forced to keep a music box playing otherworldly music concealed beneath her skirts. Another lady (thin as a rail this time), Mary Baker Eddy, maintained that she could walk on water. One can only imag-ine the strain of making sure that people took her at her word and didn't ask for personal demonstrations.... The cab-balist Mathers felt compelled to play chess with specters, which must have grown tiresome over the long haul, a true feat of endurance. All the famous mediums had to practice endlessly in private in order to achieve the desired effects at séances. You can't just lift a table with a fork hidden in your sleeve right off. So work, work, and more work.

Spirits, Stars and Charms by L. Sprague de Camp and Catherine C. de Camp, translated from the English by Waclaw Niepokolczycki, afterword by Jerzy Prokopiuk, Warsaw: Panstwowe Wydawnictwo Naukowe, 1970.

In Cold Blood

⁂

W HY AM I READING this book? I have no intention of set-
ting up a home terrarium. Let alone an aquaterrar-
ium. I don't plan on keeping either amphibians or reptiles,
however fetching. Not to mention a Caspian or Pelopon-
nesian turtle, a fettered toad, a striped toad, a clawed frog,
or a chuckling frog. Or a chameleon, which is capable of
moving its two eyes independently, e.g., one up and the other
sideways, which doubtless gives it great satisfaction. Or a yellow-
belly, though it merits consideration due to both its enchanting name and its agreeable disposition. I am tempted neither
by the salamander with lungs nor by the one called "un-
lunged," a creature that really doesn't have lungs or even gills
and still gets by. I abjure the society of the tiliqua, an Australian lizard, however rewarding it might be to find out
where it begins and where it ends, since its tail looks exactly
like its head. I forswear the snake of the Dasypeltidae family,
even though its throat contains ingenious bony growths designed to crush the shells of eggs swallowed whole. I have neither the time nor the space for this assemblage, and I suspect

I lack the kind of nerves I'd need to provide for them appropriately. I'd be forced to procure fresh-caught flies, earthworms, grasshoppers, small birds, slightly larger birds, snails, larvae, butterflies, cockroaches, and galleyworms. I know and like many of these viands. I could serve only galleyworms without regret. At least I think I could, since I still don't know what they are. In other words, I'm not this book's ideal reader. I'm reading it only because since childhood I've derived pleasure from accumulating useless knowledge. And after all, who's to say what's useless and what isn't? Take the instructions on how to mail frogs so that they arrive bright-eyed and frisky at their final destination: who knows when this may come in handy for personal or civic purposes? Adam Taborski imparts his vast knowledge about reptiles and amphibians with genuine affection. The photographs taken by Lech Wilczek sustain this high emotional standard. The map of the modern world fares worse, since it doesn't show England or Ireland. The artist just forgot about them. Perhaps he unwittingly assumed the viewpoint of the amphibians and reptiles, for whom two little islands falling into the sea naturally pales in comparison with the catastrophes of the Mesozoic.

The Terrarium by Adam Taborski, photographs by Lech Wilczek,
Warsaw: Panstwowe Wydawnictwo Rolnicze i Lesne, 1970.

THE STATE OF FASHION

ℐℛ

STUDENTS OF THE sartorial arts study (quite rightly) the history of European dress. This textbook for fourth-year students caught my eye in a display. I looked over the table of contents. The history of fashion was divided into five lofty chapters: Primitive Community, Slavery, Feudalism, Capitalism, and Socialism. I decided to read it, since how clothes took their form from the form of government was not immediately obvious to me. Unfortunately, the authors also fail to make this connection, though they try mightily. The problem is that you can't unlock dresser drawers with the key to the main gates of the city. It just won't fit. "The society of primitive communities," I read, "was classless, ergo in principle everyone wore the same kind of clothing." This "ergo" looks logical enough here—but it's already problematic by the next chapter. Because when the authors turn to the clothing of slavery, and to the class structure of ancient Greece, the student discovers that everyone wore the same clothes there too. The master's may have been new, whereas the slave got only hand-me-downs, but they all had the same peplos and chlamys. In Rome, of course, full citizens were distinguished by their togas—but by the time of the empire these were worn only on special occasions. It wasn't easy to tell a slave from a free man on the street; a slave might strut covered in gold, whereas free citizens just tossed on any old thing. Gibbon tells us that a motion once made its way to the senate proposing to abolish such scandalous spectacles by mandating uniforms for slaves. The senate threw it out—oh, not because they loved democracy, just the opposite. Slaves in uniforms would immediately recognize their overwhelming numbers....A tricky business! The influence of other factors on fashion, such as climate, historical events, moral norms, or technology, is also less than straightforward. No one has managed as yet to uncover the rules that govern these factors—why does one first dominate and then another, with varying degrees of intensity? This ignorance must be underscored emphatically. For the time being the surest, most obvious principle in the evolution of fashion is its dependence on styles in art and the modes of textile manufacture. The textbook does its job in showing this. I'm afraid, though, that its chief, neck-breaking conception prevails in its suggestions for examination questions. Pleasing themes such as "Clothing in the age of the Baroque" or "Elements of ancient fashion retained in regional costume" are forced to make way for more bombastic topics: "Democracy and the development of ladies' skirts" or "Explain the difference between capitalist and socialist fashion...." Thoughtful students will be in for trouble.

The Historical Development of Clothing, by Ewa Szyller, Zygmunt Gruszczynski, and Wanda Piechal, fourth edition, Warsaw: Panstwowe Wydawnictwo Szkolnictwa Zawodowego, 1970.

LOVE IN BLOOM

ℐℓ

THIS BOOK WAS written by a distinguished specialist in or-
chard cultivation, who has eaten the fruits of many a tree,
who's tasted India's mangoes, the durians of Thailand, Chinese persimmons, American avocados, the tree tomatoes of
New Zealand, and breadfruit from Hawaii. I suspect that, if
he wished, he could determine with the absolute authority
that derives from both theory and practice exactly what fruit
was eaten by our disobedient progenitors in paradise—was it
a banana, a quince, an apricot, or a pomegranate? The apple
is apparently most unlikely.... Szczepan Pieniazek doesn't gear
his book to specialists; it's intended for the many readers who
like to stray from time to time into unfamiliar fields of knowledge. Pieniazek yearns to engraft (perfect word!) in them a
love of fruit-bearing trees and shrubs. Unfortunately, though,
such amateurs live in a constant state of indecision. Every
book on natural science they pick up works to ensnare them
in an all-consuming passion. But each of these loves demands
absolute fealty and can't be reconciled with the others. If I fall
head over heels for fruit-bearing trees and shrubs, then I must

feel instant enmity toward the twenty thousand living creatures that threaten them. So much for my longtime affection
for elks, who consume shoots and twigs in orchards. So much
for my fondness for the equally voracious rabbit. For similar
reasons I must from this time forward demonstrate an active
revulsion at the sight of squirrels and deer. Hence from my
heart moles, mice, and bats! Begone, oh starlings, sparrows,
crows, rooks, and jackdaws! It's a little easier with insects, just
because there are so many of them; I could never be smitten
systematically with such multitudes. But I must confess that
even here I've got certain partialities that I'd have to forgo.
For example, I harbor a purely aesthetic, hence unpardon-
able fondness for the red spider, a tiny arachnid that's actually purple. I've always considered the red spider one of
nature's wittiest inventions and have given it top ratings for
insouciance and grace. And all this time it's been sucking the
best sap from plum and apple trees! But—maybe I don't have
to swear off the red spider? I can keep on loving it? Loving it
in spite of everything? Loving it even as it gnaws my healthy
apple tree, which is healthy only because the entire red spider
family was sprayed in the nick of time? Just because I can't do
otherwise?...Just because all our human love for nature is
warped by perversity and double-dealing?...

When Apple Blossoms Flower by Szczepan Pieniazek, Warsaw: Wiedza
Powszechna, 1971.

FEET AND FATE

♪

IN THE FAR EAST, dreaming of a dragon means good fortune. And, in truth, shortly after a certain ex-courtesan dreamed of a green dragon crawling into a peach-colored lake, a wealthy young lord fell in love with her sixteen-year-old daughter. It couldn't be otherwise. Even without makeup the young Chun-hiang was possessed of a beauty "that could overthrow nations." She was further graced with exquisite manners that included the art of writing verse. Unfortunately, due to her low birth, she could become only this lord's unofficial wife. And one day he abandoned her to "ascend upon a deep-blue cloud" in the distant capital, or, more trivially speaking, to make his career as a court bureaucrat. The tears and entreaties of poor Chun-hiang fell upon deaf ears. "Can ten thousand willow boughs restrain the wandering wind?"...The girl is left alone with faint hope for his return, but with a firm resolve to stay faithful just the same. And when a lustful old man tries to rape her, she prefers to go to prison, be locked in the stocks, and be inhumanly beaten. The hard oak cudgels bound with iron shatter her delicate feet. But the green dragon did not enter the peach-colored lake in vain. The young lord returns after having risen so high on his deep-blue cloud that he can settle scores with the vicious old man, free his lover from captivity, and make her his official wife at last. The written version of this fairy tale dates from the late eighteenth or early nineteenth century, and is rightly considered a gem of classic Korean literature. Some readers admire its vivid, elegant style. Others appreciate its effervescent love scenes. Still others are moved by its powerful emotions. There are those who appreciate its elements of social criticism, its compassion for women's hard lot. And then there are those who praise the tale above all for its refusal to fall back on fantasy. Such praise is based on the conviction that realism is the crowning glory of literary creation, while fantasy is a less respectable genre, an immature creature, the larva from which a butterfly is soon due to emerge.... The reading of fairy tales must be torture for such people. Each miracle must strike them as an aesthetic sin, each improbability as mere childishness. I'm sorry for them, since even the tale of Chun-hiang must give them facial tics from time to time. Take the aggressively happy ending, in which not a word is spoken about Chun-hiang's mutilated feet. Did her bones heal without a trace? Rest assured: they grew back perfectly. Chun-hiang will not be forced to hobble alongside her handsome spouse and fearfully cover her deformed feet in the marriage bed with a blanket embroidered with Mandarin ducks. For fairy tales never capitulate completely to life's truth. Just the opposite. They try at every opportunity to upstage it, to instruct it by way of their own, far superior, solutions.

The Tale of Chun-hiang, Most Faithful of the Faithful, translated from the Korean, with an introduction and notes by Halina Ogarek-Czoj, Wroclaw: Ossolineum, 1970.

Humor's Younger Brother

dᴘ

Humor is sobriety's younger brother. There's constant sibling rivalry between them. The earnest senior sibling patronizes little humor, and humor thus feels inferior, and longs in his heart of hearts to be as sedate as sobriety, but, luckily, he can't pull it off. The biographies of humorists (I'm drawing here on the notes to this anthology, but they only confirm the rule) reveal the authors' relentless, hopeless quest for seriousness. Nearly every comic writer has to his credit a few rotten novels or plays that have "fallen into oblivion," while the comic works, dismissed during his lifetime, have earned "a lasting place in literature." In all my days I've never encountered a biography that went the other way: "He produced innumerable sketches and countless farces without success, but his vivid portrayal of the lives of medieval peasants finally earned him immortality...." Strange! You see the same thing with actors. Every comedian secretly dreams of tackling a tragedy. But I've never heard of a tragic actor wailing in some café, "That moron [this is actors' slang for the director] is making me do Hamlet again! He can't get it through his thick skull that I was born to play Sir Andrew Aguecheek!"

It's truly baffling! I think seriousness and humor are equally important, which is why I eagerly await the day when seriousness will get its comeuppance and start envying humor. Humor, for example, comes in many varieties, while seriousness is never organized by categories, although it clearly should be. Dear Critics, since you employ the term "absurd humor," you should introduce its counterpart, "absurd seriousness." Learn to distinguish between forced and primitive seriousness, lighthearted and gallows seriousness. This bracingly sensical conception will jump-start critics and journalists alike. Do we not require, in life as in art, indiscriminate seriousness? bawdy seriousness? sparkling seriousness? spirited seriousness? I would read with pleasure about thinker X's "terrific sense of seriousness," about bard Y's "pearls of seriousness," about avant-garde Z's "offensive seriousness." Some reviewer or other will finally decide to remark that "playwright N. N.'s feeble play is redeemed by the effervescent seriousness of its conclusion" or that "in W. S.'s poetry one catches notes of unintentional seriousness." And why don't humor magazines have columns of seriousness? And why, moreover, do we have so many humor magazines and so few serious ones? Well?

Introducing French Humor, edited by Arnold Mostowicz, graphic design by Jerzy Jaworowski, Warsaw: Iskra, 1971.

GREAT LOVE

✑

IN THE SPRING OF 1876, shortly after their marriage, the forty-six-year-old Dostoevsky left Russia for Germany with his twenty-year-old bride. One can't really call this the beginning of their honeymoon. The writer was in fact fleeing his creditors, and planned to amass a fortune in the German casinos. This is when Anna began keeping her diary. I don't know who first christened these notes "My Poor Fedya." It gives the impression that the young wife felt primarily pity for her sickly, manic, and extraordinary spouse. Whereas Anna actually admired and approved of her unusual husband; she loved him humbly and blindly. "My Splendid Fedya," "My Wonderful Fedya," "My Wisest Fedya"—these are the titles we should pick from. Objectively, life with her Fedya was a hell of fear, anxiety, and humiliation. Subjectively, though, it made her happy. One smile or kind word was enough to dry her tears, and she'd gladly remove her wedding band, her earrings, and her shawl so that Fedya could pawn them, then use the proceeds to gamble and lose everything once again. Anything that might cheer him or bring a moment's pleasure in his troubles consoled and delighted her too. She saw the world through his eyes, assumed his views, mirrored his complexes, shared his annoying contempt for all things non-Russian. She nursed him with sinking heart when his epileptic seizures struck—and they were frequent in those years. She endured his repeated, unexpected fits of petulance, the scenes he provoked in restaurants, shops, and casinos. Anna was pregnant during this period, and it was an exceptionally difficult pregnancy, perhaps because of her perpetually strained nerves. But, as I said, she was happy, she wanted to be happy, she managed to be happy and couldn't even conceive of greater happiness....We're dealing here with the phenomenon of great love. Detached observers always ask in such cases: "So what does she (he) see in him (her)?" Such questions are best left in peace: great love is never justified. It's like the little tree that springs up in some inexplicable fashion on the side of a cliff: where are its roots, what does it feed on, what miracle produces those green leaves? But it does exist and it really is green—clearly, then, it's getting whatever it needs to survive. Ryszard Przybylski writes in his introduction half-jokingly (but he means it) that Anna Dostoevsky's diary should be a how-to book for wives: how to cope with a difficult but well-intentioned spouse. Unfortunately, her experience is of no use to anybody else. Anna wasn't following a plan. Loving forbearance was simply her second nature.

My Poor Fedya by Anna Dostoevsky, translated from the Russian, with an introduction and commentary, by Ryszard Przybylski, Warsaw: Panstwowy Instytut Wydawniczy, 1971.

BONES TO PICK

ஜ

H erbert WENDT'S NEW BOOK is a pleasant, at times rather chaotic recounting of the history of paleontology. I can't resist the temptation to retell one episode from this history. It's neither the most dramatic nor the most significant, but my pen itches just the same. So, in the second half of the past century it turned out that the northwestern part of the United States was a veritable gold mine of fossils. The territory to be excavated was vast, and what was dug up surpassed all imaginative projections. A real fever seized paleontologists generally, but two were even more seriously affected than the rest: Cope and Marsh. Both were born wealthy, and their entire inheritances went on exploratory expeditions. One day in the state of Kansas they bumped into each other for the first time and instantly felt an implacable, mutual hatred. If one was excavating in a particular spot, the other would immediately start digging there too, and both would simultaneously claim exclusive digging rights. Whatever they didn't dig up themselves they would buy from the middlemen who bounced back and forth between the two, upping the price of every tibia. Initially the paleontological rivalry of the two men sought an outlet in the scientific journals, but it soon overflowed into the daily papers. The gentlemen publically charged one another with paleontological espionage and paleontological poaching, not to mention paleontological plagiarism stemming from paleontological hooliganism with a touch of paleontological ignorance and a healthy dose of paleontological derangement. That's my jaw, Marsh bellowed. That's my tail, Cope scowled. Give me back my bones, and I won't tell you what you are, Marsh snarled. Ha! Cope scoffed. More than once they must have longed to seize the first rib that came to hand and neutralize the enemy—but unfortunately the ribs were the size of bridge spans. Scientific organizations, courts, social and political institutions, and finally the U.S. Senate were drawn into this battle over jurisdiction and rights to excavated saurians. Satirists had their hands full. After Cope died, Marsh outlived him by two brief, barren years—since what kind of life was this? The time then came to set the record straight on the two scientists. It turned out that they'd left an enormous legacy, both in pounds and in productive findings for future scholars. It cannot be determined whether they would have achieved even more by working in concert. One would have to resurrect them for experimental purposes and place them in identical circumstances, but with friendship replacing enmity. I fantasize about such comparative resurrections in thousands of different historical instances. Just think of the pedagogical benefits! Just imagine our certainty at last in the face of desired Good and permissible Evil! But since that's not possible, I must with a heavy and unwilling heart accept only such knowledge as I have been given to know: Edward Drinker Cope and Othniel Charles Marsh hated one another with great profit.

Before the Flood by Herbert Wendt, translated from the German and with an afterword by Anna Jerzmanska, Warsaw: Wiedza Powszechna, 1971.

THE SCALES OF JUSTICE

∂∬ρ

THE WITCH-HUNT THAT raged in Europe in the sixteenth, seventeenth, and even eighteenth centuries apparently claimed a million victims. Even if this figure is slightly exaggerated, it would in no way diminish the awfulness of this phenomenon. The effects of such a terror are never confined, after all, to those who perish. They also include the incomparably greater number of barbarized, physically ravaged, morally debased human beings who survive. The belief in witches escalated with every execution. Still, there were always a few people ready to protest; efforts were made, time and again, at least to mitigate this plague. We know a great deal about this age's horrors. We know too little, though, about the battle waged against them, and there was a battle: this psychosis didn't simply vanish on its own. One should remember not only the deplorable *Hammer Against Witches*. Other books urged common sense and mercy: Jan Vierus's *Treatise on Witches*, Fryderyk Spee's *Book of Conscience*, and Baltazar Bekker's *A World Bewitched*. One should bear in mind those cities and provinces blessed, at least at times, with reasonable leaders: the Republic of Venice, Paris. Other towns long resisted this mania: Augsburg, Bremen, Ulm. In Brugge a law was passed whereby any person accusing another of witchcraft was himself imprisoned and held until the charges were proved. Informers fell silent instantly. In England a ban on torture during investigations conspicuously reduced the number of denunciations. But for me the Dutch town of Oudewater shines like a star on a bleak night. The city had a public scale used to weigh cheese and flour and, upon occasion, people. Current superstition held that witches were lighter than their height and build would suggest, hence the weighing of witches was common practice in many areas, always, alas, with fatal consequences for the accused. The scale in Oudewater was thought to be infallible, a last resort. Hundreds of fugitives, persecuted, harried wretches from neighboring lands, sought it out. The weighing was performed with due ceremony, in the presence of the aldermen and local population. The mayor and city councillors would then hear the aldermen's testimony in full assembly, draw up a certificate complete with signatures and seal, and present it to the individual who had been weighed. And not a single verdict ever came out negative! The suspected witches were free to return to their homelands without fear, bearing written affidavits that their weight was exactly what it should be. The Oudewater scales still stand, a monument. May fate preserve them for all ages—along with the memory of those people who performed their lifesaving comedy without so much as a wink to hint that the outcome was fixed in advance. The people of Oudewater were both good and clever. Goodness is helpless without wits.

Witches: A History of Witchcraft Trials by Kurt Baschwitz, translated from the German by Tadeusz Zabludowski, with an afterword by Bohdan Baranowski, Warsaw: Panstwowe Wydawnicto Naukowe, 1971.

HOME IMPROVEMENT

ℐℐℳ

I DON'T LIKE THE WORD "handyman," but of course I admire the people it describes. Their atavistic gift for performing all kinds of manual tasks reminds me of primitive societies in which everybody still did everything. As it turns out, these living relics of a time before the division of labor are perfectly adapted to a time of crisis in human services. Aside from their unvanquished drive to do battle with matter, these people have preserved yet another trait of primitive peoples that is of great value today: their instinct for foraging. Every screw, every scrap of tin you glimpse on the sidewalk is worth stopping for, since if it doesn't come in handy now, it surely will some ten years hence. Others may seek out junk shops only when pressed by dire necessity; *they* drop in for inspiration and rummage among the chisels for an hour, purring with pleasure. You have to be born a handyman; you can't suddenly become one in midlife. As with ballet, you have to start practicing early; otherwise you'll never be a master. The handyman has had a flamboyant boyhood; he has learned how to balance on death's edge amid corrosive liquids, broken glass, short circuits, and experimental detonations. His parents are summoned to his school with above-normal frequency, where they discover that their son has rigged beneath the teacher's chair a device producing knocking from below. The handyman's maturation lies chiefly in the contents of his pockets being transferred to drawers. When the handyman moves to a new apartment with a convex floor and a slew of similar problems, he has years of experience behind him. You might even say he's the right man in the right place. The paean I pronounce in his honor here is loosely connected with the book *Repairing and Redecorating Your Apartment.* The handyman, with his God-given talents, would never buy such a book, since he doesn't need it. This genius has already seen somewhere how you fasten, for example, two counterweighted lugs, and to see—if only for a split second—means more to him than whole nights spent studying the theory of fastening such lugs. This book is thus intended for those credulous clods whose hearts it floods with the false hope that the first hook pounded into a wall as per its directions will be a hook well-pounded. This foray into home improvement will inevitably end with a call to a repairman, who will dolefully drag out his arrival for two weeks. And here I see the single real reason for reading this book. You can chat with this repairman with the same finely feigned air of mastery that the poet Julian Tuwim once used on his locksmith. And what good is life without conversation?

Repairing and Redecorating Your Apartment by Hanna and Wojciech Mieszkowski, Warsaw: Watra Publishers, 1971.

Nowhere to Hide

⌘

Staying at home is exceptionally dangerous; death or crippling accidents await our every step. I should add that every new, civilized convenience we acquire is yet another disaster waiting to happen. People were safest when living in caves, that is, as long as some saber-toothed tiger didn't invade while the masters were off hunting somewhere. This brochure, by A. Dziak and B. Kaminski (in an effort to economize on letters, the press doesn't give their full names), prepares us for various emergencies and teaches us how to administer our own first aid. The authors stray far beyond their titular topic in their ardor for instruction. Apart from mishaps at home, they cover accidents in the yard, the forest, and the river. And they close their useful booklet with a chapter on "Procedures in the Event of Mass Injuries (Natural Disasters, Atom Bombs)." The reader's astonishment is complete, since nothing in the book, whose dust jacket depicts a colorful house standing on a bandaged leg, had even hinted at such a conclusion. I was asked once at a reading why I write about books on popular science and how-to guides instead of serious literature. I answered that these books never turn out either happily or sadly, and that's what I like best about them. Now I see that I'll have to rethink this position. There's no way to be sure that the next book off the presses won't be a handbook on the care and feeding of infants that culminates with the apocalypse.

Accidents in the Home by A. Dziak and B. Kaminski, Warsaw: Panstwowy Zaklad Wydawnictw Lekarskich, 1970.

Who's Who

❧

ALICJA HALICKA WAS a native of Krakow who fled the family nest at an early age to study painting, first in Munich, and a bit later, in 1912, in Paris, where she married the famous cubist Louis Marcoussis and permanently joined the ranks of the Parisian avant-garde. Although she was a painter, she doesn't have much to say about her own or her husband's work; and she doesn't have anything particularly new to say about the other artists either. The teens and twenties in Paris—years of major, dramatic breakthroughs in all areas of the arts—appear in her memoirs as a series of anecdotes about famous people. Snapshots of bohemian life, well-aimed stock phrases raining down on both sides of the Seine, a picturesque parade of major and minor celebrities: it all begins to wear thin after a while. Finally you'd just like to hear about someone without a famous name, someone who'd be forgotten if not for this book. There'll be endless memoirs, after all, about the Picassos and Apollinaires.... Halicka, as they say, knew "everyone." But knowing "everyone" is a bit much, and really means you don't know anyone. You simply don't have the time or energy. The more acquaintances, the fewer friends, as we all know. She snares each new victim with a well-chosen cliché and then presses onward to another opening, a fresh premiere, a new salon....But one day illness strikes the author, who is housebound for many months. The whole burgeoning, buzzing, busy world of "everyone" suddenly disappears as if swallowed up by the earth itself, and she's left alone with the old servant who looks after her, Mrs. Dubois. And wouldn't you know, this Mrs. Dubois is the hero of the book's best story, even though she wasn't an artist or an aristocrat, just a humble ex-washroom attendant. At one time she'd done a fair amount of traveling with her lover, a croupier, and had practiced her demanding trade in various gambling dens from Cairo to Buenos Aires. When asked about her impressions from these distant journeys, she replied laconically, "Well, ma'am, I always worked in the basement, so I didn't see much...." Good Lord.

Yesterday by Alicja Halicka, translated from the French by Wanda Blonska, Krakow: Wydawnicto Literackie, 1971.

TALKING PICTURES

♪♪

T HIS BOOK ISN'T HOT off the press; it came out two years
ago. But I couldn't get hold of it back then, and I only
recently caught sight of it in a bookstore window. To live in
this world and know nothing about the Chinese alphabet
makes no sense. After reading this book I still know next to
nothing, but this "nothing" loses its primitive meaning and
acquires Socratic profundity. The book contains a great deal
of information on Chinese languages and dialects, on the history of an alphabet whose symbols designate not sounds, but
the meanings of words, on how these characters are com-
posed, and on calligraphy. The characters' composition interested me the most. Thus, for example, the sign meaning
"peace" is made up of three pictographic elements: a roof, a
heart, and a container. This is already a microscopic poem.
Chinese characters have generally forced poets to be maximally concrete. If they wanted to write a poem about a bird,
they had to decide right off what kind of bird they had in
mind. Was its tail long or short? Or did they want a third sign,
which combined the other two, but meant a large, fat bird?

There is another sign meaning a bird without any specific qualities, but the alphabet's pictorial nature retains until this day its resistance to abstract concepts. It has also kept its distaste for women. "Quarrel" depicts two female figures in graphically simplified form, and "treachery" or "betrayal" portrays no fewer than three female figures.... It goes without saying that there's one sign for "wife" and another for "lover." "Wife" is woman plus broom, while "lover" is woman plus flute. I don't know if there's a character expressing the ideal that every European woman's magazine promotes: the broom and flute together. I'm grateful to the author for both the wealth of information and its lucid presentation. It's unfortunate, though, that he spent so little time on the Chinese alphabet in daily life. I'd have liked to find out how long children have to spend in schools just learning to read and write. When do they finally achieve total recall of every character in current usage? How efficient is Chinese note-taking? And, finally, what does a Chinese typewriter look like? For the time being, I imagine it as an object the size of a locomotive transporting eighty brisk stenographers from place to place. In that case, the sign for stenographer would combine "woman" with "dragon."

The Chinese Alphabet by Mieczyslaw Jerzy Kunstler, Warsaw: Panstwowe Wydawnicto Naukowe, 1969.

GLASS HOUSES

cJfⰈ

T HE EMPEROR'S REALLY got it made...." God save us from
such deals. "At dawn his coffee is served in bed...." In
other words, the servant on the day shift enters his bedroom,
replacing his counterpart from the night shift. The emperor
could not for an instant go unwatched, unattended, and un-
guarded. The etiquette at Napoleon's court wasn't half so
strict as it was for, say, the Hapsburgs. Nonetheless, it was
unheard-of that the emperor should wash himself, comb his
own hair, and button his own trousers. He didn't even get out
of bed himself; he was gotten out. He fell from his valets'
arms directly into the waiting arms of secretaries and aides-
de-camp. When heading off to that spot where even mon-
archs must go on foot, he bypassed the various witnesses to
this event, who were standing fixed at attention or bent into
bows. When he returned to his office to do a little work in
peace, he could hear his faithful Constant's heavy breathing
just beyond the door. He must have been gifted with remark-
able concentration, since this didn't bother him. His frequent
tawdry affairs were discreetly arranged by a third party. He

couldn't ever really be by himself, just drop out of sight, cease being the center of universal attention for even a few days. Someone always had an ear pressed to his door, and it wasn't even worth yelling, "Go to hell," since that person would just step back a couple of paces. Such a life strikes me as monstrous. Anyone who thinks it would be fun to be Napoleon in spite of everything clearly has exhibitionistic tendencies. Napoleon's and Josephine's divorce, along with everything leading up to it, took place, needless to say, in view of the entire court. Josephine fainted publicly, while her ambitious spouse grew publicly pale with embarrassment and irritation. No photographer was present, of course, but Constant, the future author of these memoirs, was more than enough. I don't count Napoleon among my favorite historical figures, but even so I felt something close to pity for him after reading these memoirs, the kind of pity that a caged tiger merits. But this may not be the best comparison. The tiger paces its cage involuntarily, while Napoleon was more than happy to squeeze into his little cell. When he was sentenced to the island of St. Helena, he was no doubt tortured by his mortally injured pride, but I suspect that he probably took to the way of life forced upon him without much trouble. He was still the center of attention in his new environs, he still felt upon him the watchful gaze...of his lackey? his guard? Does it really make much difference?

The Memoirs of Emperor Napoleon I's Valet by Louis Wairy Constant, translated from the French by Tadeusz Ewert, introduction and notes by Jerzy Skowronek, Warsaw: Czytelnik, 1972.

PAGE-TURNERS

ഫ

AND WHY NOT SAY A couple of words about the kind of calendar whose pages you tear off? It's a book, after all, and a pretty thick one, since it can't have any fewer than 365 pages. It turns up in kiosks in editions of 3,300,000, and is thus the ultimate best-seller. It demands uncompromising punctuality from its publishers, since it can't be pushed back on the timetable for another year or two. It requires professional perfection from its proofreaders, since the slightest mistake might disorder minds. One trembles to think of two Wednesdays in one week or St. George usurping the feast day of St. Joseph. A calendar is not a scholarly work to which errata are traditionally appended. Neither is it a volume of poetry, where editors' mistakes pass for the whims of inspiration. It follows from all this that we're dealing with an editorial curiosity. But that's not all. The calendar is doomed to gradual liquidation as its pages are torn off. Millions of books will outlive us, and a considerable number will be ridiculous, dated, and badly written. The calendar is the only book that has no intention of outlasting us, that does not lay claim to a sinecure on the library shelves; it is programmatically short-lived. In its humility it does not even dream of being pored over page by page, but its pages brim with texts just in case. There's a little bit of everything: the historical anniversaries that fall on a given day, rhymes, maxims, witticisms (what passes for wit on calendars at any rate), statistical information, riddles, warnings about smoking, and hints on eliminating indoor pests. The dissonances caused by this appalling mishmash of material are dreadful: history's sublimities stand cheek by jowl with everyday trivialities, philosophers' precepts vie with rhymed weather forecasts, heroes' biographies condescendingly consort with Aunt Clementine's household hints.... Some will, of course, be appalled. But those of us who live in Krakow (and thus next door to kingly tombs) are moved by the calendar's ambiguities. I've even come to see a secret resemblance between the calendar and the world's great tales, as though the calendar were akin to the epic, an illegitimate infant.... And when I stumbled on a few lines from one of my own poems under one date (a good one, God willing!), I accepted this fact with mournful resignation. The other side had a recipe for Viennese cheesecake: a pound of cheese, a tablespoon of potato flour, a cup of sugar, six tablespoons of butter, four eggs, vanilla, raisins. And, ending with these raisins, I wish my Noble Readers a happy New Year.

Wall Calendar for 1973, Warsaw: Ksiazka i Wiedza, 1972.

The Long-Distance Walker

✑

T HE TOURIST ON FOOT is a person who leaves Point A and arrives at Point B by way of his own feet even when other forms of transportation are available between Points A and B. The tourist on foot reaches Point B much later than he would have if he had taken a train or bus, and at the journey's end he is far more tired, dirty, hungry, and smug. In society's eyes, this kind of tourist is comical or serious, eccentric or normal, depending on whether he travels alone or in groups. Everything's fine so long as he sticks to the group. Membership in a collective sanctifies his every step; it crowns his head with a halo of higher necessity. They walk because they must, we think on spying a sprightly troup of Boy Scouts or students with backpacks. They walk because it's good for them, because they're young, because they're on vacation. The lone tourist, on the other hand, provokes suspicion and wonder. To trudge along on foot when you could take a car or bus, to take the long way just to avoid busy highways and the temptation of hitchhiking: it's clearly insanity! This is why a person no longer young who wishes to spend his vacation wandering solo, duo, or trio at most, must constantly defend himself against family and friends. The argument that he just likes to walk meets with profound disbelief. Someone told me recently about an incorrigible solitary walker who'd won an automobile. Even that couldn't cure him. On the first day of his vacation he locked the car in a garage and set off on foot from Wroclaw to Kolobrzeg, a distance of some three hundred miles. Even his closest friends then realized that he was mentally ill. Apparently it's very easy to shock people these days. Salvador Dalí has to work like crazy to achieve a reputation for eccentricity; his stunts require costly production and advertising. The gentleman from Wroclaw shocks more cheaply and efficiently. I send him my very best wishes en route. And now for a few words about the book lying before me. The title and dust jacket both feature a tourist in the singular. However, the text demonstrates that the author is concerned with collective tourism, with various nomadic camps, rallies, jamborees, and powwows. ("A jamboree is a large powwow generally intended for some portion of a rally's participants.") The edition likewise suggests large-scale intentions, since twenty thousand copies are in print. There are many fewer solitary tourists, and their numbers are dwindling. Only in the next generation will walking, I suspect, become truly avant-garde.

Vade Mecum of a Tourist on Foot by Stefan Sosnowski, Warsaw: Sport i Turystyka, 1972.

BACK TO NATURE

❧

THERE ARE STILL virgin forests on earth known to civilized man only from the heights of airplane windows, bodies of water uncontaminated by factory wastes, air unpoisoned by chemical fumes. In short, one still can find those primeval paradises for which every other pop song pines to the sound of electric guitars. The people in these paradises live in accord with the will of Mother Nature, that is, on equal footing with crocodiles, snakes, scorpions, and locusts, not to mention all kinds of protozoans, viruses, and bacteria. Many people are preoccupied with protecting the natural environment in developed civilizations. And rightly so. But the term itself is disingenuous. What we want to preserve is an environment scrupulously purged of undesirable elements—nature unnaturalized in the most calculated way! In truly natural environments, human lives are wretched and brief. Overpopulation, famine, disease, and ignorance: these are different faces of the same elemental misery. In his journalism, Lucjan Wolanowski approaches this problem from the angle of disease. This book was commissioned by the World Health Organization, which wanted him to cover health issues and medical practices in Southeast Asia. Wolanowski must be the most highly vaccinated Polish journalist of all time, since he's always traveling to distant lands. But vaccinations can't prevent every disease. And there are no vaccinations to guarantee mental resistance. Wolanowski, who visited hospitals, quarantine sites for infectious illnesses, and densely populated areas in which epidemics rage without end, was surrounded by horrific sights. I think you'd have to possess exceptional moral courage to endure all this and suppress a shudder of disgust and horror. I recommend the book to anyone who's glanced at the jacket and thought, "He sure gets around...." And I recommend to everyone, regardless, this straightforward account of human beings suffering in a hundred different ways that we Europeans have managed to forget completely....Since nature, left to its own devices, is diabolically inventive.

Heat Waves and Fevers by Lucjan Wolanowski, Warsaw: Iskry, 1973.

FAIR GAME

❧

EUROPE NO LONGER holds large wild animals that exist beyond the reach of our good, or bad, intentions. Only
small fry escape our surveillance and may, in certain spots,
live in genuine freedom. Larger species may have the impression that they live as they please, but in reality they're subject
to remote-control cultivation. If we set to work with determination and energy, we could exterminate every large species
in two or three years, or even in five with the active assistance
of our bureaucrats. No one wants this, naturally. While reading Stanislaw Dziegielewski's book, which exhaustively covers
everything concerning deer in the past, present, and future, I
reached the conclusion that this beautiful animal will survive
in Europe as long as there are hunters. Hunters won't allow
this animal to die out, since anyone who likes hunting has to
have something to hunt. And so the hunter flips through the
pages of this book in a double role: he is both destroyer and
protector, both the exterminating angel and the guardian
angel at once. He holds a gun in his right hand while blowing
a kiss with his left. The most frequently used term in this

book, aside from "deer" and "antlers," is probably "prophylactic shooting." Prophylactic shooting improves the species,
since it eliminates clearly inferior specimens. Prophylactic
shooting pays heed to the desired ratio of male to female.
Prophylactic shooting regulates the distribution of game, so
the animals can thrive without excessive destruction of forest
and field. Prophylactic shooting even improves the deer's
beauty, hindering the propagation of specimens whose horns
grow this way and not that. In short, prophylactic shooting
acts in various ways for the deer's own good. It's just a shame
that they don't know it.

The Deer by Stanislaw Dziegielewski, second edition, Warsaw:
Panstwowe Wydawnictwo Rolnicze i Lesne, 1973.

Changing Places

ঞ৯

I T's NOT ENOUGH that we spin with the Earth around its
axis. It's not enough that we industriously circumnavigate
the Sun each year. It's not even enough that we speed with the
Sun and the entire affiliated galaxy with monstrous speed to
God knows where. As if this bizarre mobility weren't enough,
the ground beneath our feet is constantly shifting. Just look,
in 300 million years—that is, in no time at all—our beloved
Europe will be taking New Zealand's place. I submit that New
Zealand should peaceably withdraw in advance. The vision of
this voyage helps me to withstand the hardships of daily life,
even though thus far the theory of continental drift has only
been partially proven in the eyes of scientists. But it's also true
that scientists have just recently begun to conduct research
and observations. It all began in 1912, when a German mete-
orologist, Alfred Wegener, astonished the world with his claim
that continents wander across the globe's surface. At one time
they comprised a single mighty land mass, which had sun-
dered some 200 million years ago, and the pieces then drifted

apart, making room for the Atlantic. The lines of the severed coasts (western Europe and Africa contra both eastern Americas) clearly matched, and this worked to his theory's advantage, as did continuities in geological formations and affinities among Jurassic flora and fauna. But for science the assertion that "Susie has a cat" has no meaning. You must also establish that: 1) Susie is Susie, 2) the cat is a cat, 3) that any given cat may actually be the property of any given Susie, and 4) how it happened that this particular Susie became the possessor of this particular cat. Continental drift? Perhaps, but how was this to be explained? Doubt was heaped upon doubt, and some skeptics reached such a degree of refinement that even the similarity of coastlines became an argument against Wegener's theory. For how is it possible, they asked, that the severed lands could retain their original outlines for so long? Meanwhile Wegener perished amid the glaciers of Greenland and the whole affair died down and was forgotten. It resurfaced, though, in the realm of radioactivity and the earth's magnetism. New methods revealed that England and Ireland had turned thirty degrees to the northeast from the Triassic age to the present. And that the Scandinavian peninsula was stubbornly rising at a rate of one meter every hundred years. And that the direction of earth's magnetic pole changes at a constant rate, and the ocean's floor retains a complete record of these changes... We may still hope, say the authors of this book, for further revelations in this century. Geology, they assert, stands on the threshold of a major breakthrough, just as astronomy did before Copernicus and Galileo, as biology did before Darwin, as physics did before quantum mechanics. The vision is fascinating in and of itself, so long as humanity doesn't discover the laws that govern the motion of the earth's surface and then figure out a way to slam one land mass into another.

Continental Drift by H. Takeuchi, S. Vyeda, and H. Kanamori, translated from the English (since no one could handle the Japanese) by Jedrzej Muller, Warsaw: Biblioteka Problemow, Panstwowe Wydawnictwo Naukowe, 1973.

Blowing Your Own Horn

♪♪

Recognition, admiration, and ever-growing fame greeted Louis Armstrong from the age of twenty on. His celebrity was entirely deserved, but it was difficult to bear in daily life. The modern Orpheus doesn't have to be torn apart by harpies. Their place has been taken by the fans lying in wait at club entrances and exits, the journalists and photographers, the autograph seekers, the professional and amateur Peeping Toms, the hosts of "friends and relatives" demanding financial assistance and favors, the blackmailers, psychopaths, and schemers. The charming, good-natured Satchmo—even he was forced to defend himself from his own popularity by erecting a wall of secretaries, and perhaps even a bodyguard with mighty biceps, in order to work in peace.... This is naturally very aggravating, and makes a person bitter. Then of course the world sees that its idol's gotten bitter and holds it against him. His old pals, who remember the idol from the early days, find this particularly unforgivable. They shake their heads sadly, knowingly: the guy's full of himself, it's gone to his head, same old story. I can't shake the impression that Armstrong wrote (or, rather, dictated) his memoirs with these people in mind, hoping to cajole and mollify them. Hey, listen, all you out there in New Orleans—he seems to say on every page—black and even white, living and even dead, my head wasn't turned, I didn't forget you, read and be satisfied that I have a kind word for everyone, even though you know yourselves that it's not always true. And most of all you, my musical pals for whom things didn't always work out—not only do I give your names and nicknames, I pay solemn tribute to your musical gifts, sometimes even greater than my own, and if I know anything at all, I picked it up from you. I just had better luck, which bothers me a bit, and so I humbly ask your forgiveness just in case.... Such is the memoir's tone. Noble and touching. But is it sincere? Oh, let's not be petty, seeking sincerity in memoirs doesn't make much sense. It's worth asking what version of his self and world the author's chosen—since there's always room for choice. You may reach for your pen, for example, just so as not to have a single good word for anyone.

My Life in New Orleans by Louis Armstrong, translated from the English (very well) by Stefan Zondek, Krakow: Polskie Wydawnictwo Muzyczne, 1974.

THE ROAD TO PERFECTION

ઈપ

HATHA YOGA IS A system of breathing and movement exercises that originated in India. Regular practice (an hour daily, or fifteen minutes minimum) is said to yield splendid results insofar as we are able to achieve the required concentration, that is, to withdraw from the external world. Hatha Yoga eliminates conditions of exhaustion and nervous tension, and leads over time to the full development of the personality. It is not, however, for everyone, as the title rashly promises. People who are exhausted and overwrought don't have time for exercises, and people who have time for exercises are without doubt not especially exhausted and overwrought. Moreover, Hatha Yoga is not for skeptics, since skeptics withdraw only with the greatest difficulty. Withdrawal requires a willingness to believe and a little advance enthusiasm. The skeptic who has completed exercise number twenty-five (the so-called Kukkutasana), who is, that is to say, sitting on the ground with legs somewhat parted, bending the right leg with hands clasped beneath the foot and crossing it over the right side of the groin while inserting the right hand be-

tween the calf and thigh of the bent leg, will still manage to
think in an unacceptably secular and worldly fashion, "What
is it I'm actually doing anyway?" Next, as he extends the left
leg with the help of the left hand while grasping it (the leg)
with the free hand, placing the foot on the right leg, inserting
the left hand in the same manner between the left thigh and
calf, bringing the foot as close as possible to the left hip, join-
ing the palms, which are resting on the ground between the
bent legs, touching the thumbs, bending the rib cage forward,
inhaling, rising, and removing the body from the earth in
such a way that it rests only on the palms, and breathing nor-
mally for a moment in this position, he remains riddled with
doubts as to whether his personality truly benefits from this
corporeal macramé. He then realizes that Hatha Yoga is only
the first small step on the road to perfection, and this perfection, according to the Hindu sages, will be achieved only by
those who lose their individual I in the Cosmos at large. Here
the skeptic stops to ask himself if this is really his business.
Maybe just the opposite: he shouldn't lose himself, but simply
live his life through in its human separateness with all the
consequent difficulties? And as for losing himself—there's always time for that after death. At this moment the skeptic begins to disentangle himself from the Kukkutasana. We hope
he'll succeed without the help of paramedics.

Hatha Yoga for Everyone by Halina Michalska, second edition, Warsaw:
Panstwowy Zaklad Wydawnictw Lekarskich, 1974.

TROUBLE IN PARADISE

ℐℛ

I N 1937 THE TWELVE-YEAR-OLD Helena Valero was abducted under dramatic circumstances by the Yanoama Indians, who lived in the forests between the Rio Negro and the source of the Orinoco River. After twenty years she managed to return to her native civilization, and her story (as transcribed by an Italian ethnographer) is a unique ethnographic and psychological document. At the time, whites knew almost nothing about the life of the Yanoama. And the Yanoama in turn did not seek contact with white people. Isolated by a primeval wilderness, they dwelled in their own "airtight" reality, submerged in what civilized people call prehistory. The only foreign object they knew was the machete, a blade devised for cutting vegetation, which they had acquired by way of occasional exchanges made along the riverbanks. In their hands, however, it did not become an instrument of death, a sinister symbol of so-called higher culture. The tribes of the Yanoama decimate one another by way of their own conventional weapons: clubs and poisoned arrows. Which are so effective that the women's fertility rate does not offset the losses occasioned by the men's belligerence. What prompts these intertribal wars, wars without beginning or end? They aren't caused by basic needs. The tribes do not know hunger; hunting grounds and building materials abound. And still they perish—or this at least is the impression I took from this astonishing book. A certain custom seems to be to blame, a custom so strong that it supersedes all the other customs this culture has forged to insure its continued survival. From boyhood the men ritually inhale a narcotic called "epena," obtained from local plants. The smoke powerfully enhances their aggressiveness, and after a certain point seriously affects the mind. The women of the Yanoama know that when their husbands, brothers, and sons gather to inhale epena that violence is sure to follow, since a motive always turns up after a few deep breaths. The honor of each man rests upon his becoming a "waiteri." A waiteri is a man who has killed a man who previously had killed several other men. Hence the idea of the knight-errant extends throughout the community. We know of similar knights-errant from our own Middle Ages, but these were simply individuals looking to while away the dreary days between wars. Whereas every Yanoama man must be a waiteri, which casts the future fate of these tribes into doubt. The people appear to be paradisiacally healthy; there are almost no diseases (do they even live long enough to get sick?). Are we perhaps dealing with some form of mental degeneration? Were all prehistoric hunter-gatherers governed by similar laws? Then how did they survive? What caused these laws to evolve? The questions are naive, but when face to face with Her Majesty Anthropology I'd rather not pretend to know what I don't.

Yanoama: The Story of a Woman Abducted by Indians by Ettore Biocca, translated from the Italian by Barbara Sieroszewska, Warsaw: Panstwowy Instytut Wydawniczy, 1974. This copy was borrowed, since the minuscule edition vanished instantaneously.

Zuzia

♪♪

DOMESTIC BIRDS DIFFER from poultry in that we keep them in cages for aesthetic pleasure. Our own, of course—I don't know anything about the pleasures of birds doomed to live with their owners on permanent display before them. The book describes eighty-eight different birds that tolerate life behind wire bars reasonably well. Each description is enlivened by a colored illustration depicting the male. The females are omitted, even though their appearance is very different from the male's in some species. This beautifully produced book inspires one to take up bird-breeding, but anyone who actually takes the first step under its influence will have to take the shopkeeper's word for it when buying females. I recently wrote about an album on butterflies that was similarly prejudiced against caterpillars. I won't say that it's complete nonsense, though it's close. But let's get back to the birds. The birds which imitate the human voice comprise a particularly winsome group. My luck has been such that I've never yet heard a "talking" starling, let alone a parrot. The only parrot I got to know as a child could not be persuaded to speak. The house's female inhabitants tried to get it to repeat polite expressions such as "good day," "good night," "bon appetit," and "thank you." Whereas the men were at the same time encouraging Zuzia (that was her name) to learn various phrases less suited to the parlor in which her cage hung. The unhappy parrot, caught between two hostile systems of education, refused to say a word to the end of her (brief) life. She did, however, react to the clock. She'd fall into a fury as soon as it began to strike the hour; she thrashed her Technicolored wings and emitted a terrible shrill, yet guttural voice that horrified me. I can still hear it clearly today. I was only seven or eight back then; you don't think about time passing at that age. One hour ends, another begins, and so what? But Zuzia, it seemed to me, was a creature who took such matters to heart. She shrieked as if trying to scare off something that can't be frightened, or at least as if protesting something that ignores our protests. "What we do battle with is so small, what battles us is so large," Rilke wrote. I read Rilke much later, though. First there was Zuzia, who just couldn't stand the sound of the clock.

Domestic Birds by Jiri Feliks, translated from the Czech by Barbara Bzowska-Zych, illustrated by Dagmar Cerna, Warsaw: Panstwowe Wydawnictwo Rolnicze i Lesne, 1974.

LILLIPUT LOST

✒

T HIS BOOK ANALYZES the interdependence between a body's dimensions and its vital functions. The smaller the animal, the quicker its metabolism; it thus also has more rapid respiration and heartbeat, greater voracity and higher fertility. When exceptions to this rule occur, the author tries to explain their subsidiary cause as scrupulously as the guiding rule itself. I venture to suggest that this work will disappoint neither learned zoologists nor laymen seeking knowledge of the natural sciences. They will have much to suffer in the name of that knowledge, though. I myself, for example, had hitherto been convinced that the fantasticality of Swift's Lilliputians derives from the fact that there are no Lilliputians, and there are no Lilliputians because they don't exist. Now I have to make peace with the thought that they don't exist because they're completely impossible. It's a major difference, a fatal blow to the very idea of elves! The author gradually builds up to this blow. First he asserts that the Lilliputians unnecessarily overfed Gulliver. They thought that insofar as he was 1,728 times larger than a full-grown Lilliputian, he must therefore consume 1,728 times more food. Whereas Gulliver could actually have gotten by on 144 Lilliputian portions per day. On the other hand, the Lilliputians themselves would have had to eat far more frequently than they do in Swift's story. Not three, but thirty-six meals daily, with a combined weight equal to one-fourth of their own total body weight. Otherwise they would quickly die of hunger. The necessity of procuring such large quantities of food rules out a civilized way of life, the cultivation of refined customs, and higher education; it calls into question the existence of chefs, bookkeepers, gardeners, and architects, and makes all culture impossible. Humans could create culture only because they are relatively large organisms with a slower metabolism and, as a result, have a fair amount of spare time at their disposal, without which culture doesn't stand a chance. The ruthless author thus denies the Lilliputians the right to a civilized kingdom. As if that weren't enough, he also denies them access to a human form of movement. The matter of Gulliver among the giants fares no better. Such gargantuan bodies would, for a variety of reasons, be forced to live in the water and comport themselves in accordance with the exigencies of a liquid environment. In short, a human being can only be a Gulliver among Gullivers.... To soften the blow, I'll add that only within the—exceedingly narrow!—limits of this species could he expend the energy necessary for reading Swift and his splendid fable.

Giants and Dwarves of the Animal Kingdom by Everhard Johannes Slijper, translated from a German translation by Stefania Jarzabek and Mieczyslaw Kowalski, Warsaw: Wiedza Powszechna, 1975.

DIVAS

❧

EVEN IN THE SIXTEENTH century a woman playing a woman's part was considered shocking in a respectable theater. Boys dressed as women—say, a sweet cross-dressing little Desdemona tangled up in his petticoats at Othello's side—were another matter. As a new musical genre that arose at the same time, opera also complied with this dubious form of decorum. The shepherd Daphnis declared his love to the non-opposite sex, to which the shepherdess Chloe responded in a passionate falsetto. But by 1600, a woman was actually featured in the title role at the grand premiere of *Eurydice* in Florence. Such a scandal was possible only at a distance from papal Rome, where women would still be long forbidden from appearing on the stage. With time this Roman edict became more and more difficult to enforce, since opera was thriving and the demand for boy sopranos kept growing, while the supply was limited and in constant danger due to the inevitable changing voices. Hence they began to castrate them. Whatever it takes to protect public decency... Thereafter the roles of ethereal nymphs, shepherdesses, and divinities were played by obese, overgrown invalids with inhumanly beautiful voices. All the opera houses in Europe began to compete for them, even those in which women had already been more or less accepted. Castrati became fierce competition for the fairer sex, whose members were therefore often confined to the roles of sentimental, amorous young men. This created a situation straight out of a carnival sideshow. One London production featured as many sopranos in pants as castrati in crinolines. This may have been marvelous aurally, but it must have been monstrous visually. When the barbarous crippling of young boys finally ceased, the women had a chance to recoup their losses, since they both inherited the castrati's female roles and retained their earlier men's roles. The arrangement was thus close to what it had been originally, but in reverse: the sleeping (operatic) Desdemona was menaced by a female, artificially mustachioed Othello. Chopin witnessed just such a production in Paris. The Othello was tiny, whereas the Desdemona was built like a house, and Chopin quaked, thinking that the strangling might take place in reverse. I always admired him for not letting Mickiewicz talk him into writing operas. No doubt he had more important reasons for sticking to the piano, but who knows, his tremendous sense of the comic may have entered the picture as well. He could foresee all kinds of casting catastrophes that he would be helpless to avert. And he could already see himself, the unhappy author, cringing in the darkest corner of his box.

Nightingales in Silk and Satin: From the Lives of the Great Prima Donnas by Walter Haas, translated from the German by Juliusz Kydrynski, Krakow: Polskie Wydawnictwo Muzyczne, 1975.

THE PSYCHIC LIFE OF PETS

ઝ

I N THIS BOOK ON canine illnesses we find discussions of virtually all the complaints that trouble people, from anemia
to yellow fever. Dogs suffer and die from the same causes as
humans. They try to keep us company even here. They suffer
far more discreetly, of course; they don't describe their every
pain, they aren't prone to exasperating hypochondria, and
they don't abbreviate their lives by smoking tobacco and drinking vodka. This doesn't at all mean that their health is statistically better than ours. Apart from the illnesses we share,
dogs are also afflicted by specifically canine ailments. The
book runs to four hundred pages with good reason, and
would seem to be an exhaustive account of its subject. But it's
not. The author omits the most common canine problems,
namely, all kinds of neuroses and psychoses. Early veterinary
medicine ignored this, but interesting research is now being
done on the psychic life of pets. It's too bad that there's nothing out there we can read on this. We'd surely find out that
our Rexes and Rovers don't have an easy time of it. They
spend their whole lives trying to understand us, to adapt to

the conditions we impose, to catch the drift of our words and gestures as it pertains to them. It's an enormous strain, endless stress. A dog is filled with despair every time we leave the house: we may be gone forever. Our return is bliss bordering on shock—some miracle has preserved us. These farewells and greetings touch us, but we should also be appalled. When we leave for several weeks, we have no way of telling the dog when we'll be back; we can't cheer him from the road with a postcard or long-distance phone call. The dog is doomed to an eternity of hopeless waiting. But this isn't all. There are a hundred other situations in which the dog may lose his equilibrium while endlessly juggling the demands of his own nature and the foreign human world around him. Finally, sooner or later, he begins to chase his own tail, which is not, so we are told, a harmless pastime, but a sign that our ward has lost touch with reality. Among humans, who lack tails, this stage of the disease remains asymptomatic.

When Your Dog Gets Sick by Peter Teichmann, translated from the German by Wladyslaw Kermen, Warsaw: Panstwowe Wydawnicto Rolnicze i Lesne, 1974.

THE NINETY-POUND WEAKLING

❧

I N ITS FINAL CHAPTER, the how-to book *Increase Your Strength and Agility* warns against the development of excessively bulbous muscles, but I'm not sure how sincere this advice is, since the book's illustrations show only bodybuilders. All appearances to the contrary, I'm not adverse to bodybuilding. I've got nothing against smooth or striated muscles. Bruno Miecugow is certainly much less sympathetic than I when he claims that bodybuilders are precisely the missing link that anthropologists have been fruitlessly pursuing, shovels in hand, in various cracks and fissures. I, on the other hand, do not think of bodybuilders as the missing link. They're exceptional precisely because they begin life as ordinary people and achieve their bulk only by dint of titanic exertions and sacrifices. Such, for example, was Max Sick, future king of bodybuilders, who started out as a scrawny schoolboy, a target for stronger kids. And Sandow? Sandow was snubbed by a girl who told him point-blank, "Your skinny arms and sunken chest disgust me." I suspect that we would find women and schoolboys playing a fiendish role in the stories of other bodybuilders as well. The spurned Sandow quickly set to work on his rib cage and extremities. After several years of weight lifting he became an athlete. What happened to the girl? History is silent on this point. Did she throw herself, chastened, into Sandow's waiting biceps? As far as I know life and its propensity for jokes at our expense, everything turned out completely differently. Shortly after this episode, the girl married some ordinary weakling just because she fell in love, and, as we all know, love is blind. And while Sandow was busy doing squats and alternating right and left leg lunges while horizontally extending the opposite arm, the ingrate was bearing her spindly spouse three children, enthralled that they all came out looking like their dad. Finally, though, while pondering Sandow's fate, I ended up sincerely liking him. The maniacal determination with which he built up his muscles (inter alia, the deltoid, the gluteal, the front dentoid and the large pectoral, the oblique abdominal and the anterior tibial) didn't do the slightest harm to anyone, and that's got to count for something in this less-than-kindly world.

Increase Your Strength and Agility by Stanislaw Zakrzewski, fourth edition, Warsaw: Sport i Turystyka, 1976.

Do It Yourself

JP

"THE ENTHUSIASM FOR wallpapering your home yourself"—and I quote—"has not bypassed our country, and
the last few years have witnessed mounting enthusiasm for
this practice among home-owning handymen. It now ranks
among those hobbies clustered under the heading of 'Do it
yourself....' " Well, fine, but half of the heading has been
chopped off. In its entirety it would read: "Do it yourself since
you can't count on the experts." Hobbies in their Polish vari-
ant are pastimes taken up not voluntarily, but by necessity.
Such hobbies are not really hobbies at all, and should we
really bother introducing foreign words into Polish that have
no meaning here? If you decide to go ahead and wallpaper
your place regardless, then by all means read this book and
consider what awaits you. First of all there's the business of
finding the right tools. Two or three of them can usually be
found around the house, while more specialized equipment
must be borrowed or bought. Scouring the stores will easily
(or, rather, not easily) take two weeks at the least, counting
evenings after work. You will visit some stores several times,

since they haven't got it today but may have it tomorrow. Taking your cues from this book, you will also drop by the paint store, where, we are told, they lend tools with a deposit, but in reality they don't. You will spend your time after dinner visiting your friends, since, who knows, they may turn out to have this or that. It's not polite to strike like lightning; you've got to bring candy for the kids and ask about the parents' health and general well-being. Sometimes you accidentally stumble upon somebody's birthday or something along these lines and return home only at four in the morning without even managing to ask about the putty knife and paint roller. Other times the only person there is the deaf grandmother, who doesn't know anything. It goes without saying that the visit must be repeated in such cases. So let's add another week. If after its passage you still lack a complete set of utensils, you must undertake several trips both in and out of town. So let's say yet another week. Then, having all the necessary gear in hand, you can finally think about purchasing the various glues and putties and, of course, the wallpaper itself. Let's tack on another week. Now at last you can begin the preliminary labors: moving the furniture, covering the floors, scraping and leveling the walls, and preparing various mixtures. Another week, if not more, in dishevelment, dust, and despair. I won't go into the actual techniques of wallpaper application; I'll add only that they are very complicated and time-consuming for anyone who lacks experience. The wallpaper in the second room will certainly look slightly better than it does in the first room—assuming, of course, that you have a second room. The entire mess will consume close to two months. During this time all your other work will lie fallow, and it will take another month for you to catch up on past business, not to mention, à la "do it yourself," fixing the window broken while you were wallpapering your home. There's just one thing you can't restore, namely, that priceless chunk of life. You've wallpapered it all and then some, but you're exhausted, depleted, demented, and depressed. You're civically, culturally, and philosophically deprived. A whole lifetime may fly by in this fashion. And it does, it does.

Wallpapering Your Home by Jan Wojenski, Warsaw: Watra, 1976.

To Be Continued

ॐ

THE HORROR ROMANCE, otherwise known as the Gothic novel, was a popular literary genre in the second half of the eighteenth century in England. People devoured them for the same reasons that we read detective fiction today. The action never faltered, and terrible dangers lurked at every turn. The tales invariably came equipped with half-ruined castles, cellars, dungeons, rocky caverns, and forests filled with bands of ruffians, whose eyes were invariably wild and whose garments were rank. The tales were likewise incomplete without villainous counts, mysterious penitents, masked avengers, and foundlings. Fortunately, every foundling bore some special sign upon his shoulder blade or at least wore some medallion, thanks to which he could at some point preordained by the author come into possession of his rightful name and inheritance. Phantoms, skeletons, and ominous dreams were also highly regarded, as were daggers on which blood shed many years earlier still appeared to be fresh. Virtually all the aforenamed elements converge in *The Italian*, which is thus a worthy representative of its genre. I doubt, though, that it will still be read with goose bumps. Still I found it immensely moving. As a child of eight or nine I stumbled upon a similar book and read it rapturously. It couldn't have been *The Italian* (this is the first Polish translation), but it was something in the same vein. I remember the book itself—it looked just the way it should, having come down through a couple of generations. It was missing its title page and cover, the pages had frayed edges and bore the yellowed prints of many fingers; it held a dried violet, a fly flattened over time, sums done in the margins and doodles executed in crayon by some child I didn't know. I still remember the despair with which I counted the remaining pages. Finally the cruel moment came when I had to read "The End." Beyond these words yawned a void that I yearned to fill at all costs. So of course I decided to write my own novel. I set to work energetically; I sharpened my pencil and opened a blank notebook. I didn't have to rack my brains over the heroine's name, I already had one on hand. From some magazine or other I remembered a picture titled "Idyll in the Garden." It showed a pair of lovers against a rosebush, but I thought that Idyll was the girl's name. So the first sentence of my novel read as follows: "Brown-eyed Idyll gazed off into the horizon from which the mailman would arrive bearing a letter from her betrothed...." Then the action began in earnest. Someone crept up to Idyll from behind, and a monstrous paw fell heavily upon her shoulder. Here, unfortunately, the text breaks off for unknown reasons. And now I'll never know what would have happened next.

The Italian, or the Confessional of the Black Penitents by Ann Radcliffe, translated by Maria Przymanowska, with an afterword by Zofia Sinko, illustrated by Barbara Ziembicka-Soltysik, Krakow: Wydawnictwo Literackie, 1977.

How Not to Be Noble

JP

I̲T'S REALLY MAINLY about the first half of the seventeenth century. The second half didn't leave much time for daily life in all its splendor; history kept upsetting its rhythm. The authors don't deal with historical facts in their book; they aren't concerned with assigning blame to the nobility for the way things turned out. Instead they describe and analyze the nobility's estates, their families, their way of life, their income, their administrative service, their education, their mind-set. You get the impression that everything may not have been irreversibly, irretrievably bad in the upper classes. It goes without saying that being noble was a nasty business—not just in Poland, but everywhere. The nobility had roughly the same aspirations, horizons, tastes, and gestures every place they turned up. Polish lords weren't the only ones whose steeds strode shod in golden horseshoes. They weren't the only ones to compete with one another in palatial magnificence, culinary extravagance, and funerary splendor. Kondrusz's banquets were no less outrageous than the Radziwills'. Apparently, then, our noblemen were not different from anyone else's. But it's worth asking whether everyone everywhere practiced exactly the same type of profligacy. Unfortunately they did not, and at this point the thread of resemblance begins to unravel. I read somewhere about a banquet arranged by a senator from Genoa for Karl IV of Hapsburg. The expensive utensils from which the emperor deigned to eat and drink were flung into the sea, accompanied by a fanfare of trumpets. A gesture worthy of the Polish nobility—but what followed was no longer Polish. Invisible nets had been spread beneath the sea's surface, and the abandoned riches were raised from the watery depths the next day. We Poles lacked both literal and metaphorical nets. Our gestures were too serious. And there is yet another, far graver difference. I'll bet that most of the utensils from the Genoan feast, along with the furniture, gowns, statues, carpets, musical instruments— in short, virtually everything—were the work of native artists and craftsmen. And even though these people weren't always rewarded as they should have been, still their existence was valued and supported. Here in Poland no one ever bothered to stimulate and develop local production. Everything they had was imported from abroad. If it had been technically possible, they would have imported entire prefabricated palaces. The vision of a palace gliding in from abroad very likely haunted the dreams of more than one sleeping nobleman. Swoosh, swoosh, swoosh, over mountains, rivers, fields, mowing down forests, crushing half-starved villages and towns along the way, drawing closer, growing larger every moment, a brand-new, ready-made palace, its windowpanes glinting sweetly in the sun. In the palace a hundred rooms, and in every room, Persian rugs, Flemish hangings, Italian paintings, and on every table goblets of Venetian glass are bobbing...

The Daily Life of the Polish Nobility in the Seventeenth Century by Wladyslaw Czaplinski and Jozef Dlugosz, Warsaw: Panstwowy Instytut Wydawniczy, 1976.

FOR EVERY OCCASION

꿇

"FLORISTRY..." This relatively young and feeble little word has already incurred numerous obligations. Reference will be made here not only to floristry proper, that is, the art of floral arrangement, but also to the weaving of wreathes and the plaiting of garlands, that is, to wreathery and garlandry, terms soon destined to enrich our onomatological stockpiles. One might add to this new research in the field of vasonry, that is, the selection of suitable vases, and pottistry, that is, the cultivation of potted plants. But this isn't all. The authors enlarge their subject's scope by way of disquisitions on geometry, optics, composition, diplomacy, and ideology. So it's not surprising that there are so many authors—no one could have tackled this alone. It has been translated in its entirety, unabridged and uncut, including a substantial chapter on the organization of the flower trade in the German Democratic Republic, with detailed prices, graphs, and tables, even though most of the data were gathered at least ten years ago and are clearly passé. I am indebted to this chapter for its creation of the pleasant, if illusory, impression that there are no paper shortages in present-day Poland. The book would be harmless enough if it kept to professional information, of which it contains a fair supply. Naturally I have nothing against the whiff of exoticism that emanates from foreign customs and tastes. I read about "the artist's wreath," for example, with some amusement. It reveals that our neighbors to the west have retained the delightful tradition of bestowing garlands upon inspired persons. "On such occasions a medium-sized Roman wreath is covered with green or golden laurel leaves which require no further adornment." Still, the sportsman's wreath speaks more powerfully to the heart, since "oak leaves secured to a band create a more stirring effect than the Roman wreath." I was also touched by the floral bridal muff, a practical notion, since most weddings take place, after all, in winter. The authors generally place strong emphasis upon the representative role of flowers in personal, professional, and political life. With this in mind, they advocate the exclusive use of "refined," that is, cultivated, flowers. The non-hothouse hoi polloi hold no charm or value for them. Wildflowers, in their opinion, are suitable only for "indiscriminate" children. The humor is enhanced by a dust jacket depicting a nosegay of flagrantly wild flowers done up in peasant fashion. This is either a tacit polemic on the authors' taste, which I doubt, or the usual publisher's faux pas, which I believe.

Floristry by S. David, K. Deutschmann, M. Freitag, A. Hofmann, J. Kamp, H. Linke, M. Lobst, E. Miessner, translated from the German by Aleksandr and Marcel Wyrwinski, Warsaw: Panstwowe Wydawnictwo Rolnicze i Lesne, 1978.

FAMILY AFFAIRS

❧

CLEOPATRA IS A Greek name. It was hereditary in the Greco-Macedonian dynasty of the Ptolemies, who ruled Egypt after the demise of Alexander the Great's empire. There were seven dynastic Cleopatras, but only one, the seventh and last, would make a dazzling career for herself in a posterity she didn't know. Her precursors sank into oblivion. One might think that they led quiet, uneventful lives at the sides of their royal consorts, brothers, and sons. Nothing of the sort. An uneventful, quiet life is a luxury that none of these ladies desired, and they couldn't have had one even if they'd tried. The times were turbulent, the winds were strong and gusty from various points of the compass, and thrones were shaky. And add to this the family arrangements so difficult to comprehend today! The Ptolemies adopted the tradition of the Pharaohs, who imitated the divine siblings Isis and Osiris by marrying their sisters. These were not unions in name only. Just the opposite. Their goal was mutual offspring. The offspring would in turn marry each other in order to produce the next generation. Thus the mother simultaneously became her children's aunt, while their father was their uncle. Obviously this means that the son was his father's nephew, the daughter was his niece, and ditto for the mother, while being at the same time their own siblings and cousins. This complex web was partial compensation for their dearth of ancestors, since these children, though having, like us, two parents, possessed just two grandfathers instead of four, two great-grandfathers instead of eight, and so on. Even though surprises could suddenly pop up. As they did with Cleopatra VII, the famous one. She had two grandfathers, two great-grandfathers, but then suddenly four great-great-grandfathers. Had some alien blood infiltrated the primal family bedchamber? No, no, it was still the same select few, just with a little crossbreeding beyond the call of duty. So once upon a time there lived Cleopatra II, who first married her older brother, and then, after his death, her younger brother. Her younger brother, unsatisfied by the charms of his widowed sister/sister-in-law, did not wait for her death, but took as his second bride her daughter from her first marriage, that is, his own niece on both sides and, let's not forget, his stepdaughter. This young lady immediately became her own mother's sister-in-law (as the wife of her brother) and the many children she bore to her uncle/stepfather (as the brother and husband of her mother) gained in the person of their father a great-uncle (as the brother of their mother's father), not to mention that they were both their grandmother's grandchildren and nephews. I lack the strength to pursue this further (the book has a genealogical chart for such purposes), but this should suffice to show how one little family scandal doubled the number of Cleopatra's great-great-grandfathers. Although it's not that simple, since her great-great-grandfathers on the spear side were also her great-great-grandfathers on the distaff side. Insofar as the division into male and female lines still carries any weight here. From this we draw the logical, if not pressingly topical, conclusion that incest, in spite of its seeming simplicity, is a fiendishly complex perversion.

Seven Cleopatras by Anna Swiderkowna, Warsaw: Wiedza Powszechna, 1978.

On Your Toes

JP

ONE HUNDRED MINUTES for your own beauty? Every day? You can't always indulge in such luxuries, my dear vain, dizzy, professionally employed, married friend with children. And even if you could, a quick perusal of this book would convince you that one hundred minutes is just the beginning. This job is twenty-four hours, around the clock. Your personal appearance should never leave your mind even when your mind's on something else. When walking, you must watch how you walk, while sitting, how you sit, while lying, how you lie. Even while standing in line, my friend, you must stand in a manner enhancing your health and beauty. To this end, and I quote, "Press your heels together, spread your toes to the width of your fist, extend your head upward from your shoulders...." And so on, until you reach the counter, place your purchase in your bag, and depart. But take heed, and again I quote: "Leaving the line should also serve as an exercise in correct posture. Walk with your head proudly held high, your rib cage extended, starting each step from the hip, not from the knee." Do not be gladdened by the thought, though, that upon returning home you may abandon your shopping posture for a more relaxed position. The extension of the bust must be maintained, and further obligations descend upon that proudly elevated head. I quote: "While carrying something into the kitchen or from one room to another, place it on top of your head and support it with alternating right and left hands." If you happen not to be carrying anything, cross your arms behind you and walk taking four normal steps, four steps on your toes and four on your heels; keep this alternation up as long as possible. It is also desirable that "at every free moment" the neck muscles be exercised by a soundless but pronounced opening of the lips as if pronouncing the vowels o, u, i. To a husband perturbed by the above, you must simply explain with a gently smiling face coated with strawberries or sour cream, that you are doing this for him, so that he will always have an attractive, young-looking wife. You should be in bed no later than ten, lying supine with your arms stretched lengthwise. Your husband will initially try to wrest you from this sarcophagal pose, so beneficial for the muscles, tendons, and spine. After a couple of weeks, though, he'll leave you alone, and after a few months he'll move out of the house, thus leaving you more space in which to enhance your daily routine with jogging and long-distance jumping. And do you know whom he'll move in with, that husband? With Bozena, who begins steps from her knees, stands in line with slumped shoulders, and, can you imagine, looks her age...

One Hundred Minutes for Beauty by Zofia Wedrowska, fourth edition, Warsaw: Sport i Turystyka, 1978.

CHILDHOOD AND BEFORE

♪

A SUBJECT LIKE THE childhood of animals requires at least seven volumes of four hundred pages each. Since nothing along these lines is likely to turn up in the bookstores any time soon, I greet Maria S. Soltynska's little book with open arms. The author did her best to pack her ninety pages with as much general and particular information as possible on the exceptionally odd phenomenon known as childhood, or, more precisely, puppyhood, kittenhood, chickhood, and colthood, to say nothing of what I'll call larvahood, and so on. I'd like to stop here for a moment and ponder the oddity of childhood. Or, more specifically, ponder what is oddest about this oddity. The oddest thing is probably that nature came up with childhood so late in the game. For hundreds and millions of years life came into being by way of unicellular animals which reproduced through fission. Fission can't be called birth, since it's still the same cell, which suddenly splits into two identical specimens. And it's difficult to say that these twins are the original cell's children, since you can't be your own child, you can't be transformed without a trace into your own offspring. Literally without a trace. In dividing, the initial cell simply vanishes. But it's not what other, more complicated animals know as death. As in every decent criminal investigation, a corpse is required to establish a death. But where on earth is the corpse here? It reminds me of my old school pal the protozoan paramecium. I used to think it was just some boring thing I had to sketch for unknown reasons in my notebook. I was unimpressed at the time by its means of reproduction. So it divides, so what? The question of whether my friend Malgosia S. and I would be able to sneak in to see the forbidden "drama of passion and duty" then playing at the Pastime Cinema was far more engaging and enigmatic. The paramecium claimed its rightful place in my imagination only much later. The things that nature cooked up way back then! It created something that lives, but isn't born per se and doesn't exactly die. And if it does die, the death is caused externally, and takes the shape of an unfortunate accident. It isn't inescapably preprogrammed, an inner necessity of the organism. It's as if death were merely taking the occasional odd job before moving on to a full-time position. One might conclude that paramecia and similar animalcules regularly rub shoulders with immortality. For reasons known only to itself, the evolution of living beings began to abandon its original concept and move on to the production of mortals, whose lives divide into distinctive phases that always occur in the same order: birth, childhood, maturity, old age, and death. I don't know why it turned out this way and not otherwise, and those who do know also don't actually know.

The Childhood of Animals by Maria S. Soltynska, Warsaw: Krajowa Agencja Wydawnicza, 1978.

OLD FRIENDS

ℐℐ

S AMUEL PEPYS HAS BEEN my good friend since 1954, that
is, from the second edition. Since then I've read through
this wonderful two-volume book several times; it's wonderful
partly because its author was writing for himself and wasn't
worrying about whether it was wonderful or not. He also didn't
anticipate that his daily notes, written in an easy style free of
any far-fetched figures of speech, would be translated some
day into other languages. Including Polish, and what Polish,
Mr. Pepys, what Polish! There are good translations, very good
translations, even excellent translations, and still they remain
translations. But Dabrowska's pen has occasioned that rare
miracle when a translation stops being a translation and becomes—how on earth do I put this?—becomes a second original. When this fourth edition came out, I started leafing
through it, and something strange happened: I began to wonder if Pepys was really my old friend after all. And, more
generally, if there really are friends whom you know so well
that you can comprehend the intentions behind their saying
this or that. For example: a minor episode from 1669. To cele-
brate his birthday Pepys and his family set out for Westminster

Abbey, where they visited the kings' tombs. They viewed, among other things, the embalmed corpse of Queen Katherine, the wife of Henry V. Pepys took it in his arms and kissed it on the lips. Not out of some sort of necrophilia, God forbid, but from pure, if indiscriminate, joie de vivre. "For the first time in my life," he exclaimed, "I've kissed a queen." For the first time! What optimism! A dead queen is fine for a start, but maybe some living queen will turn up down the road? Pepys's remarks always tickled me, and they still do. But up until yesterday I was convinced that his humor was absolutely unintentional. Today I don't know. Maybe his jokes were conscious after all; perhaps he's mocking himself and his purported success in higher circles. And it's a critical difference: are we laughing at the author or with him, behind his back or to his face, against or in accord with his intentions? The example I've given to illustrate my doubts may be trivial, but the problem itself is significant. How should we approach old texts? How can we avoid reading them with an indulgent, superior smile that they may not deserve? Especially when the author is not noted for his wit and only manages to crack a joke now and then. Even then his witticism either will not be understood or will be considered unintentional, something that just slipped out in spite of him. Generally speaking the passage of time creates exceptionally bad acoustical conditions for humor. I suspect there are untold victims among individual words, sentences, passages, and even entire works. The eminent scholar of ancient culture Margareta Riemschneider claims that, for example, the biblical story of Jonah was originally a comic folktale; it was meant to be funny. Only later did someone reinterpret it, misunderstand it, take it seriously. And so it remained. Just think what's happened to Homer, this same lady contends, so many jokes, winks, jabs converted into stately, noble phrases. Growing deaf and blind to what's gone by may just be the natural order of things. But that's no reason for giving in.

Diary of Samuel Pepys, two volumes, translated from the English, selected, annotated, and with two introductions by Maria Dabrowska, fourth edition, Warsaw: Panstwowy Instytut Wydawniczy, 1978.

THE MYTH OF POETRY

✑

MIODRAG PAVLOVIC belongs to the middle generation of Serbian poets and is considered a major author. As far as I know, his poetry has not yet appeared in Polish translation. The reader must therefore read his collected thoughts on poetry in isolation from the poetry itself. This isn't easy, and it's less helpful than it would be the other way around: first the poems and then everything else that went with them. It's hard to guess the furniture's shape from the blocks and chips in the carpenter's workshop. In any case, I personally pick up such poetic notebooks with a certain reluctance. I rarely come across a tone and sense I find convincing. Something irritates me about the ease with which poets write about poetry. They write as if poetry still held some secrets absolutely inaccessible to other genres. Poets have always been disposed to treat poetry as if it were the alpha and omega of literature, and of course there have been periods that confirmed this conviction. But it's old hat today. Poetry lives on, and it's certainly not a minor genre. It seems tactless to me, though, to grant it some kind of indisputable superiority in perception and feeling vis-à-vis literary prose or drama. For a long time now those who've earned it ride along on the same Pegasus, and it's not always clear who's hanging onto the mane and who's got the tail.... Poetry this, poetry that, poetry the other... In most sentences like this the subject could be replaced by prose and it would do just as well. I employed this procedure while reading Pavlovic's reflections, perhaps against the author's own intentions, but in keeping with the current state of affairs. Thus in the title chapter on myth and poetry, for example, I kept remembering what he'd left out. Works that continued ancient legends, like Mann's *Joseph and His Brothers* or Joyce's *Ulysses*. Or works that created powerful new myths, like Kafka's *Trial* or Beckett's *Waiting for Godot*. One little essay entitled "An Outline of the History of Future Literature" deserves special mention here. A dazzling piece, full of wit, although it's anything but cheerful when you come to think of it. I read it with relief, though, since finally literature is treated as a whole, and poetry as one piece of it, neither more nor less important than the rest. And that's just about the size of it.

Myth and Poetry by Miodrag Pavlovic, translated from the Serbian by Joanna Salamon and Danuta Cirlic-Straszynska, Krakow: Wydawnictwo Literackie, 1979.

In Praise of Birds

❧

I LIKE BIRDS FOR THEIR flights and non-flights. For their diving into waters and clouds. For their bones filled with air. For the waterproof down beneath their feathers. For the claws that disappeared on their wing tips, but were preserved on their feet, with the exception of paddle feet, which also deserve our best regards. I like birds for their stick legs or bowlegs coated with scales that may be purple, green, or cerulean blue. For their smart, stately strutting, but also for the hobbling that makes it seem as if the earth is never motionless beneath them. For the staring little eyes that see us completely differently. For their conical, scissor-shaped, curved, flattened, long, or short beaks. For their feathered jabots, plumes, cockscombs, ruffs, frills, doublets, pantaloons, fans, and dickeys. I give equally high marks to the grayness of birds' plumage, which is never monotonous, and to their motley, which during the mating season always manages to display itself to new effect. I like birds for their nests, eggs, and the gaping reptilian maws of their chicks. And finally for their twittering, trilling, gurgling, grating, and mellifluous voices. The author of this avian atlas gives these voices an extraordinary amount of attention. For example, "psst psst tik tik" is the come-hither voice of the gray flycatcher, whereas "bit bit tsyt crr" is the mourning flycatcher's mating call, which rules out amorous hanky-panky even between the members of such close-knit families. Obviously "translating" bird voices into the sounds of human speech is ipso facto imprecise, and it would be much better simply to include a few records with the atlas. But Jan Sokolowski knew what he was doing: given the brisk clip of our recording industry, an atlas with records might come out, say, in seventy years. For this reason his laborious, if imperfect, transcript deserves our gratitude—and it's also worth noting that he's continuing a venerable literary tradition. Since we're talking about literature, I also like birds because they've been fluttering their way through Polish poetry for centuries. Not all of them, unfortunately. The nightingale is the champion habitué and favorite of poetry. The eagle, raven, owl, swallow, stork, dove, gull, swan, crane, lark, and cuckoo likewise belong to the elite. Sightings of the heron, thrush, bullfinch, wagtail, chaffinch, blackbird, and a score of other birds do occur, but more rarely. Our poetry passes over still other birds in silence, but only because their names are so uncouth that they'd ruin the lyrical mood. I've yet to spot a single grackle, bunting, brown thrasher, or bearded titmouse. The unlucky goatsucker is no less lovely than the swallow, but has had no career in poetry. We can only hope that some future poet will at last take pity on one poor widgeon or another. But this is not the worst fate, since at least there's some hope, whereas birds with ambiguous names are doomed from the start. The chat, the stilt, or the kite would muddy the poetic landscape. The redhead shares its name with certain members of our species, and all is thus lost. Any poet who wrote, "I cast my eye about and swiftly spot, / A flock of redheads winging to my hut," would be considered a skirt-chasing braggart today. And the booby? "When all alone I mourned my desperate plight, / I spied the blue-faced booby in its flight…" I don't think so. And what about coots? "Look, love, how bright above us shines the moon, / Whilst sing the coot, the peewee, and the loon…" What bard would risk his reputation on the like? Whether these avian pariahs take their absence from our poetry to heart is another matter. They can always cheer themselves up by counting their appearances in the poetry of some other language, where their names can't be taken for anything else.

Birds of Poland by Jan Sokolowski, with colored charts by Wladyslaw Siwka, Warsaw: Wydawnictwa Szkolne i Pedagogiczne, 1979.

GLADIATORS AND OTHERS

⁀

GLADIATORIAL BATTLES began as sacrificial duels to the death held at funeral ceremonies, and probably came from Etruria. But the energy, inventiveness, and social importance they achieved later on made them a distinctively Roman form of entertainment. So Roman, in fact, that when the empire fell, they, too, closed up shop. Thus Michael Grant's book, which describes the history and rules governing these scenes of carnage, concludes with a happy ending of sorts: Rome ended, the games ended, and there aren't any Romans around now for us to get mad at. I'd suggest taking a broader look at this issue. The gladiatorial battle was essentially nothing more than a form of public execution. And humanity has devised a fair number of such forms over time. We're better off getting angry at all of humankind from its birth up until our own sweet century. Even the ingenious merging of the penitentiary system with the entertainment industry was not original to the Romans. Primordial forms of execution, in which the captured enemy or criminal was killed on the spot and then eaten, didn't lack for crowd-pleasing features. They

weren't carried out just any old way; they were celebrated
with triumphal pomp, with joyful leaps, bounds, applause,
and melodious wailing. Later, a certain amount of progress (I
wish you could see me wincing as I write this word) was made
vis-à-vis condemned prisoners, not all of whom were executed right away; some were saved for sacrifices on major
feast days. But these postponed executions didn't lose their
entertainment value. Just the opposite—it grew. There was
now time for painstaking advance preparations. Specially
trained troupes of dancers, singers, and musicians took part
and the site was fittingly arranged and decorated. Everyone
dressed in their Sunday best for the sacrifices; hawkers with
baskets of fruit and pastry made their way through the
crowds, and infants wailed in the arms of their absorbed
mothers, while larger children clustered on the branches of
nearby trees. This all took place while goats were still grazing
on the hills of Rome—and it went on in much the same way
after stray cats had occupied the Colosseum's ruins. One
could write a score of books about executions staged as festi-
vals occurring at predictable intervals. Let's recall how, during hangings, quarterings, or burnings of prisoners in public
squares, head upon head would be thrust out of wide-open
windows, how balconies would collapse beneath the weight of
spectators, how guillotinings never ran short of voluntary onlookers. I have only one further bone to pick with the Romans. That such a great literature paid so shamefully little
attention to the moral side of the games. That such a patriar-
chal nation saw nothing amiss in the way that the captives
driven into the arena might include blood relatives, that fathers might be forced to do battle with sons, or brothers with
brothers. That this society, so proud of its legal system, could
happily stomach the sight of a murderer who could save his

life, or at least prolong it slightly, only at the cost of committing yet another murder. Only Seneca wrote of the games with revulsion and horror. And Tertullian and Augustine—but these were already Christians. The other critics came from Greek literature, but even these were few and far between. Of course we're free to believe that there were a few more texts that just haven't come down to us. Anything's possible.

Gladiators by Michael Grant, translated from the English by Tadeusz Rybowski, introduction by Andrzej Ladomirski, Wroclaw: Ossolineum, 1980.

Bringing Up the Rear

ॐ

T HIS EXHAUSTIVE TEXT is meant primarily for historians: students, teachers, and scholars specializing in related issues. In any case, it's not for poets. Poets don't derive much profit from such books. That is, they profit, but not in ways that the learned author intended. Everything I say from this point on is not a critique of the book, but an explanation of why I can't write such a critique. The poet, regardless of education, age, sex, and tastes, remains in his heart of hearts the spiritual heir of primitive humanity. Scientific explanations of the world don't make much of an impression on him. He is an animist and a fetishist, who believes in the secret powers sleeping in all things, and who is convinced that he may stir these forces with the help of a few well-chosen words. The poet may even have seven cum laude degrees—but at the moment when he sits down to write a poem, his rationalist school uniform begins to pinch beneath the arms. He wriggles and wheezes, undoes first one button, then another, and finally leaps out of his clothing completely, to stand exposed before all as a savage with a ring through his nose. Yes, yes, a savage, since what else can you call a person who talks in verse to the

dead and the unborn, to trees, to birds, and even to lamps and
table legs, except perhaps an idiot? So what can a poet like this
get out of the natural sciences? Zoologists turn themselves inside out trying to show us that a horse is a horse and a
chicken is a chicken and their mental states can't be explained by reference to the human psyche. Since they haven't
yet thought up appropriate terms that might suitably render
this distinction, they resort to quotes. Hence animals don't
think, they "think," they don't decide, they "decide," and so
on. The poet is so retrograde, though, that none of this gets
through to him. Show me a single poet who uses these precautionary quotes in describing his own dog. The poet's dog
is still just intelligent, and the "intelligent" ones are those who
don't share this opinion. But let us return to the subject of
history after this protracted introduction. The poet is com-
promised by his backwardness in this area as well. The past
for him remains a history of wars and concrete individuals.
Whereas for today's historians, especially those preoccupied
with constructing grand syntheses, wars and individuals are a
secondary concern at best. For these historians, the prime historical movers are the means of production, the conditions of
property-ownership, and the climate. Sporadic events don't
play a major role in the historical process. You may either
bypass them completely or present them in such a way that
they don't distract the reader from more important matters.
Phrases specially furbished for such purposes assist him here:
"the achievement of supremacy," "the loss of domination,"
"the suppression of separatist tendencies," "the sudden ham-
pering of development," and so on. Blood doesn't drip from
such words, the sparks of fires don't scatter from them. It's no
longer a treacherous assault, ambush, slaughter, rape, and re-
pression. It's simply that country X "found itself within the
range of foreign invaders" or, better, "of newcomers" or, better

yet, "within range of the culture of Y." The language of historians strives for abstraction and has largely achieved it. When
they speak of "migratory movements," it's difficult to guess
whether they mean the peaceful settlement of new territories
or the panic-stricken flight of one tribe under attack by another. Unfortunately the poet still thinks in images. On reading, for example, that one group's agricultural plans "came
into conflict with their neighbors' interests," he immediately
envisions chopped-off heads tossed into wicker baskets. Moreover, the instinct common to all primitive creatures whispers
that these baskets were woven by blind slaves, who were captured and blinded during the course of some earlier "conflict." It goes without saying that the more distant the times
under consideration are, the easier it is for historians to
achieve this immaculate and sterile style. The historian calmly
leafs through *Gilgamesh*, that most ancient epic of humankind,
and immediately latches on to what he needs, i.e., "one of the
earliest testaments to the formation of the state leadership's
social base." The poet isn't equipped to relish the epic for
such reasons. *Gilgamesh* might just as well not exist for him if it
holds only such information. But it does exist, because its titular hero mourns the death of his friend. One single human
being laments the woeful fate of another single human being.
For the poet this fact is of such momentous weight that it can't
be overlooked in even the most succinct historical synthesis.
As I say, the poet can't keep up, he lags behind. In his defense
I can only say that someone's got to straggle in the rear. If only
to pick up what's been trampled and lost in the triumphal
procession of objective laws.

The History of the Near East in Antiquity by Julia Zablocka, Warsaw:
Ossolineum, 1982.

CATHERINE THE NOT-SO-GREAT

⌘

THIS FRENCH HISTORIAN has undertaken a backbreaking task. He's decided to scrape the tar off the fiendish Catherine de Medici, whom her contemporaries saw as Satan's spawn incarnate. Huguenots and Catholics alike shared this view, the former out loud and the latter in whispers, or vice versa, depending on which camp felt ill-used by the queen at the time. By the end she was blamed for every calamity befalling France. This was, of course, an exaggeration. Catherine was at fault only in certain specific instances. This is not quite enough for a she-wolf from the Apocalypse, but still too much for this wayward lady to become anyone's favorite historical heroine. Yet this is precisely what the author has in mind. He ascribes virtues to her that somehow never managed to surface even once during the course of her thirty-year reign. He calls her the "Italian Montaigne" (Lord have mercy) and "an artist who lent her creative gifts to the realm of politics." Seven civil wars that she either couldn't or wouldn't avert don't speak well of her artistry. It's worth remembering that France wasn't the only country struggling with the problem of warring faiths. All the leaders of Europe were gnawing on this tough nut. Persecution, riots, stakes, and burnings were virtually universal. The fact remains, though, that the whole matter took the bloodiest, most bestial turn in France, which at the very least leaves us wondering whether Catherine was exactly the right person in the right place. The two camps reached an agreement shortly after her death, when another ruler had taken matters in hand. So I'm not convinced by the superlatives with which the author deluges Mme de Medici. A question mark might be placed after each one. "A splendid royal mother"—who caused her children to quake with fear, and who couldn't subdue their mutual fraternal enmity? A ruler "with unerring political instincts"—who instigated the Saint Bartholomew's Day Massacre without anticipating either its immediate or its long-term consequences? "A master of diplomacy and politics"—whom under the pressure of events the author must later reclassify as a "misunderstood woman." The strongest point in Catherine's defense is that she managed to save the French throne, which was important for the country. Yes and no. The Huguenots were also royalists willing to defend the throne. Republican ideas began to spread among their ranks only after St. Bartholomew's Day. The throne that Catherine had saved began to incubate a tiny cockroach, a deathwatch, which slowly, imperceptibly set to work.

Catherine de Medici by Jean Heritier, translated from the French by Maria Skibniewska. Warsaw: Panstwowy Instytut Wydawniczy, 1981.

THE COURTIER'S INFERNO

cJP

I N HIS WORK, EVERY memoirist leaves behind a better or
worse likeness of the people he knew, alongside two self-
portraits. The first of these two is painted intentionally, while
the second is unplanned, accidental. It goes without saying
that the first is more flattering than the second, and the second is more faithful than the first. The better the writer, the
more attention we should pay to this discrepancy.... The duc
de Saint-Simon was not an angel of justice at the court of Ver-
sailles, although that's how he thought of himself, and that's
the part he played. He doesn't overlook a single weakness,
fault, mistake, or deception in portraying his contemporaries.
Still, he allows us to catch him in the act as he flagrantly
schemes, plots, preens, grovels, backstabs, baits traps, sues for
the slightest reason, and sows fear among less canny souls.
But I'd rather be the defense than the prosecution. Ultimately he was a product of a court that had no use for his ex-
plosive energy and talents. As we know, Louis XIV lured his
mutinous nobility into a golden cage. He himself governed

with the help of his bourgeois bureaucrats while creating fictitious posts for his nobility, titles or countless privileges that had nothing to do with the real work of governing and carried no real responsibility for anything. It was a stroke of genius in the short run that later proved to be fatal—fatal precisely for his beloved monarchy. The idle nobility began at this point to chafe at the senselessness of their empty existence. Saint-Simon understood this charade, so ominous in its consequences. Yet he couldn't resist taking part in it just the same. He did exactly what vexed and amused him in others: he squawked, but stayed put, rolled his eyes, but bit his tongue. Once I copied out a line from La Bruyère: "The court gives no pleasure and makes it impossible to find pleasure elsewhere." It might be the motto of these memoirs. So maybe we should come at this comic drama from a different angle? Maybe certain natures absolutely require court life? Maybe Louis was simply doing his frustrated underlings a favor by giving them the opportunity to vent their energies in the horrors of sham ambitions and the tortures of protocol? There are people, after all, who are really only happy when they're unhappy. Or maybe that isn't it either? Let's cut Louis some slack—he didn't invent the whole spectacle of court life, after all, he just gave it a particularly effective shape. Courts existed before him and after him; they exist now and they'll continue into the future. And let's not confine Saint-Simon, a splendid writer, to his epoch alone, when his study embraces all times and races, all types and states, all countries and customs. Personally speaking, I don't believe in any hell in the afterlife. But I do believe in the wide variety of hells that people construct for themselves or others. A scholarly typography of these hells is long overdue. The hell described by Saint-Simon belongs to the genus of self-chosen hells and the subgenus of self-service hells. Its seats are filled with volunteers, each of whom ladles pitch into his or her own cauldron.

Memoirs, Saint-Simon, second edition, translated from the French by Aleksandr and Maria Bochenski, with an introduction by A. Bochenski, Warsaw: Panstwowy Instytut Wydawniczy, 1984.

THE ART OF DESTRUCTION

ᴊᴘ

THIS IS ONE OF THOSE books that describe ancient cultures and peoples on the basis of archaeological excavations. It goes without saying that I don't object to the new information, or at least the greater detail, that this popularizing genre keeps digging up. But I find myself thinking more and more often about a book that remains unwritten and unpublished—at least I haven't come across it yet. All the archaeologists and historians I've encountered summarize the problem that intrigues me in a single sentence: "The city was captured and destroyed at such and such a time." That's just it: destroyed, but how? We use the faintest traces to re-create more and more precisely how the temples looked, how the palaces were laid out, how the walls once ran. We find out more and more about the successive inhabitants of these once-splendid cities forgotten over time. We understand ever more perfectly how they were built, where the materials came from, and how long the whole process took. No one addresses, though, the means by which such cities were leveled to the ground. The walls didn't shatter at the touch of a finger, after all. It took some physical effort, some technical know-how, some tools to help them along. It required a certain amount of time, during the course of which one might come to one's senses and reconsider a hundred times—but this happened very rarely. Then finally it demanded some organized groups of people who'd decided or been forced to undertake this task. Naturally, certain preliminary labors occurred spontaneously. The enemy entered the city and plundered whatever he could. The rest he smashed, battered, trampled, and crushed. In the confusion a fire invariably sprang up somewhere, and the rest of the potential plunder fell prey to the flames. Along with the inhabitants' corpses— this goes without saying. These accidental fires weren't always effectual, though. This is why some excavations, as, for example, in the ruined city of Mari, have turned up the remnants of fuel carefully gathered at strategic sites. If the walls didn't choose to crumble even in a mighty conflagration, then doubtless still other methods were applied. They were shattered with rams, pulled down with ropes, or heaven knows what else. Even ancient Jericho didn't fall from trumpeting alone. Today it's thought that the trumpeting was intended to muffle the sound of digging. Thus trumpets may play a major role in a given city's conquest, but its demolition requires additional labors. Such as? A river was directed right through the center of captured Sibaris, for one example. Carthage presents the most interesting case though. It was razed so scrupulously that the soil could afterward be plowed. Here truly nothing was left to the destructive powers of time and nature. The work was done thoroughly and thoughtfully. Experienced, disciplined crews must have labored under the supervision of highly qualified specialists. If we turn a blind eye for a moment to its causes, we must admit that the job in and of itself was beautifully executed. It turns out that labor as such, sheer toil, sleepless nights, the sweat of one's brow, efficiency and perfection, is still not enough to guarantee universal admiration. I think this is the conclusion that the book I'd like to read would reach. I even have a title for it: "Homo destructor." This definition might enter into common currency and take its place alongside similar terms, such as Homo sapiens, Homo ludens, Homo faber. A book bearing this title would have to be fairly thick.

The Mysteries of Palaces and Temples by Bernhard Jacobi, translated from the German by Leonia Gradstein, Warsaw: Wydawnictwo Artystyczne i Filmowe, 1983.

Cosmic Solitude

✒

LIFE IS PICKY AND demands a mixture of highly specific conditions; we've found their fulfillment on our planet and nowhere else so far. Which doesn't mean that among all the billions and billions of stars there's no chance of a similar combination. Of course there is, and Olgierd Wolczek, a popularizer in the fields of astronomy and astronautics who died just recently, dedicates his book to explorations on this topic. Books of this sort inspire mixed feelings in me. I admit that I find the question of life beyond Earth quite interesting, but still I'd prefer not to have it settled too quickly and definitively. For example, I'm cheered, not disappointed, by the virtually certain fact that there is no life on any other planet in our solar system. I like being a freak of nature on our one and only, extraordinary Earth. Furthermore I'm not waiting for any UFOs, and I'll believe in them only when one comes up and pokes me in the ribs. Besides, I don't even know what I'm supposed to expect from them. They may just be planning an inspection of bristletails, caddis flies, and trematodes. The conviction that if they were so inclined they would lend a hand with everything strikes me as hopelessly banal. At the turn of the century, fashion called for rotating tables at which you could summon up the spirit of Copernicus to tell you who'd stolen your garnet ring or the spirit of three-year-old Sabina, who'd authoritatively predict when and where to expect the next European war. It was taken for granted that every spirit must know everything and be good at everything. But why am I writing about whether or not I believe in UFOs? It looks rather tactless when discussing a book that keeps strictly to the facts and draws upon them exclusively in reaching its cautious conclusions. Who knows, maybe I'm doing it because the belief in UFOs has its serious side: fear in the face of cosmic solitude. I don't mean to make light of this, I'll just try to ask a few questions. Would this solitude really be so awful? So unbearable? So "wretched and repulsive," as the author himself defines it at one point? Would we really be driven to darkest despair by the news that life doesn't exist beyond Earth? Oh, I know, I know, no scientist will make such an announcement either today or tomorrow, since we have no data at this point and no way of obtaining data in the imaginable future. But let's stop and think about such a revelation. Would that really be the worst of all possible news? Perhaps just the opposite—it would sober us, brace us, teach us mutual respect, point us toward a slightly more human way of life? Perhaps we wouldn't talk so much nonsense, tell so many lies, if we knew that they were echoing throughout the cosmos? Maybe a single, other life would finally gain the value it deserves, the value of a phenomenon, a revelation, a specimen unique to the entire universe? Every stage manager knows that the tiny figure of an actor against the backdrop of dark curtains on a vast and empty stage becomes monumental in every word and gesture....And after all, would the solitude we fear so much really be so solitary? Along with all the other people, plants, and animals? Can you really speak of a solitude so complex and varied? I'll add one more thing: the thought of the Earth's biological solitude has also occurred to several contemporary astrophysicists. Not many, I'll grant you, but a few. They may be mistaken, but what an intriguing mistake.

Man and Others Out There by Olgierd Wolczek, Wroclaw: Ossolineum, 1983.

THE IMPRESARIO

⨎

I HAVE BEFORE ME A splendid monograph that treats the life, times, and work of the artist in an expert and engrossing fashion. William Hogarth undoubtedly does not belong among the top ten portraitists of all times (although even Goya would not be embarrassed by his "Girls with Shrimp"). Neither is he an outstanding landscape painter, since he didn't paint landscapes at all. The realm of historical painting wasn't foreign to him, although if he'd kept strictly to this genre, he'd have achieved little fame either within his lifetime or after it. Hogarth's renown stems chiefly from his series of engravings and oil paintings conceived in a satirical, allegorical, and mock-heroic vein. These works are so fused with his age (that is, the first half of the eighteenth century) that we still see it through Hogarth's eyes. Thanks to Paulson's monograph we recognize yet another of his claims to fame: he was a peerless organizer of artistic life in England. He was instrumental in enacting the first law in the domain of author's rights. He achieved great feats in the training of young artists. Yet if we needed to sum up his achievements in one sentence, we'd have to say that Hogarth created a public for the fine arts. English literature, theater, even the relatively new field of journalism—each had its own public. But art? Of course there were artists, there were commissions, purchases, and even earnings. Then the made-to-order objets d'art vanished either into the homes of the wealthy, where only guests invited for roasted piglet could observe them, or into public institutions, where clients scanned the walls absentmindedly, or finally into churches, where true believers admired the splendid interiors with meek simplicity of spirit. None of these are publics in the modern sense of the word, the sense that Hogarth understood so well. He required not just clients, but fans, not just the opinions of a few connoisseurs, but the interest of relatively prosperous burghers and even the curiosity of plebians. Like no one before him, he exploited the possibilities of newspaper advertising: he announced subscriptions for future etchings; he printed notices for auctions, lotteries, and exhibits; and he exhibited wherever he could, even in theaters, restaurants, and hospitals. This was all new then. He had both friends and enemies. He provoked the latter into open polemics. His master plan concerned more than just selling paintings. Before Hogarth "arose," court taste, which valued only imports, prevailed in England. Paintings from Italy or Holland were the most highly prized. English artists were commissioned to make copies, or, if they were lucky, to paint portraits in the fashionable Italian style. Thanks to Hogarth and his countless enterprises, "true portraits of Englishmen" began to emerge in England. The accusation against him ran that everything he did served only his own interests. In reality, everything he did, he did for other artists; he paved the way for them, showed them new possibilities, strengthened their sense of self-worth. I should add that he kept coming up with marvelous ideas until the day of his death. For one exhibit he hired a man to stand guard before his painting and jot down all the spectators' comments. If he'd lived just a little longer, he'd have hit on those souvenir booklets now displayed in museum lobbies. He and a group of friends also arranged an exhibit of old London signboards, the equivalent of a naive art show today. Court recognition came late, when he had no use for it. He was registered on the Lord Chamberlain's list as a court painter with a yearly salary of ten pounds. He gave far more than that away to charity. The royal rat exterminator, who was next to him on the list, received forty-five pounds annually. And rightly so. This is an unpleasant, hopelessly temporal job, with no prospects for posthumous glory.

Hogarth: His Life, Art, and Times by Ronald Paulson, abridged (and she shouldn't have) by Anna Wilde, translated from the English by Halina Andrzejewska and Zofia Piotrowska, Warszawa: Panstwowy Instytut Wydawniczy, 1984.

CLOSE CALLS

ঞ৷ৎ

I DON'T REMEMBER ALL the impressions prompted by my first reading of Montaigne. In any case, surprise wasn't among them. The existence of this work, the living voice with which it continues to speak—I took these for granted. What foolishness. Now the existence of anything good fills me with astonishment. And since the *Essays* are a good thing (even one of the very best that the human spirit has achieved), everything in them amazes me, especially the exceptionally propitious mix of circumstances that made their writing possible. It wasn't at all unlikely, for example, that an infant of the male sex christened Michel might have died shortly after birth. The mortality of newborns was such a common phenomenon back then that no one even looked into the numerous possible causes. God gives and God takes away, and the potential gifts of one tiny dead child would have remained an undiscovered mystery. The boy survived: but every hour, every week, every year, he might have been stricken by various deadly diseases whose names would take up several typewritten pages. And unfortunate accidents? The little Montaigne might have fallen from a tree, a horse, down the stairs, he might have been burned by scalding water or choked on a fish bone, he might have drowned while playing in the river. Such mishaps, moreover, are not confined to children. Additional traps also await an adult, such as, for example, duels, tavern brawls, an overnight stay at an inn that someone accidentally set on fire. The religious war then raging in France was the main reason, though, that these essays might never have been. There was no room for neutral positions here, and there wasn't so much as a mouse hole in which you might wait out the storm. The tempest lasted too long and passed through the entire country more than once. Montaigne sided with the Catholics and even took part in several campaigns against the Huguenots. There's no evidence, though, that he participated with the requisite partisan ardor. Neither of the warring camps could contain his critical intellect. The danger he faced was no less for this. Just the opposite—he was under fire from both sides at once. In this maelstrom, though, it was possible to perish regardless of your opinions. Let's take a look. We see a waning autumn day, the sun has already set. Two horsemen, a traveler and his servant, are returning home along a forest highway. They're difficult to see, it's foggy, and the night is upon them. Suddenly several shots fly from the thickets, we hear a cry, the neighing of frightened horses, the crack of branches, and the racket of the perpetrators fleeing into the forest's depths. The traveler on his rearing horse spreads his arms and plunges headfirst, lifeless, to the ground. Oh, sorry, silly mistake: someone else was supposed to be heading along this road at just this time. It's not the worthy Mr. Michel Montaigne whom the terrified servant shakes and tries to revive in vain. The victim was past thirty, nearing forty, and had just begun to plan his magnum opus. Fresh paper and an ink pot with a sharpened goose quill were waiting for him in the turret of a small castle. Perhaps the first sentences had already blackened one of the pages.... So how can we not be amazed that the *Essays* came into being? That they appeared in their original form while the author was still alive? That the edition, moreover, wasn't burned along with its printer? There's nothing easier, after all, than finding a thousand disloyalties in a writer who thinks for himself. And, finally, how can we not be amazed that the numerous corrections to the already published work, which comprise the final form of the *Essays* as we know them, weren't forgotten, lost, stolen? That they were preserved and added to the next edition three years after the author's death? I therefore recommend that the *Essays* be read with astonishment. If fate had thwarted their creation, doubtless some other work, or several works together, would have become the highest intellectual standard of the sixteenth century. We wouldn't have a clue that they'd achieved this lofty ranking by way of an ordinary walkover. There are no empty spots, after all, in the dense fabric of history. Or, rather, there are—there's just no way to prove their existence.

Essays by Michel de Montaigne, three volumes, translated by Tadeusz Boy-Zelenski, edited, with an introduction and commentary, by Zbigniew Gierczynski, Warsaw: Panstwowy Instytut Wydawniczy, 1985.

What's the Mystery?

∽

YOU DON'T HAVE TO BE an expert in any field of knowledge to write a book like this. You don't have to travel the globe and seek out personal contact with those who've witnessed various astounding events. There's absolutely no need to follow up on what's going on with Miss Clarita in Manila who supposedly was battered and bitten by some invisible individual in broad daylight before a crowd of spectators. In order to write this kind of book, you need to read other books along these lines and then update them with the latest information taken from the tabloids. Then you have to shuffle everything, divide it up, and tell it in your own words in order to avoid charges of plagiarism. Naturally some sensations fall prey to the passage of time. In the sixties, for example, you no longer find the headline accounts of people abducted to the moon and their fascinating conversations with its inhabitants. But then something new always turns up. The Yeti now has brethren in every dense forest in the world, the Loch Ness monster turns up in every deep lake and fjord, and aliens are so abundant that you have to take great pains not to slam the door accidentally on one. Harsh words directed at science are a hallmark of such books. Science is shockingly dismissive and indolent, it is blind and deaf to the proofs presented to it, proofs that it always finds either false or insufficient. But there are even worse menaces than science. Several photographers who managed to take pictures of spacecraft know something about this. Shortly thereafter three men dressed in black forced their way into the darkroom and demanded the pictures in broken voices, after which they departed in a black limousine without license plates. The reader may think that I'm a thick-skulled rationalist who can't even entertain the idea that anything strange, mysterious, and amoral could still happen on our ordinary earth. It's just the opposite—for me there is no such thing as an "ordinary" earth. The more we find out about it, the more mysterious it is, and the life it holds is a bizarre cosmic anomaly. A tree that grows with leaves that rustle—this is enough to astound me. I don't require any Jurgenson with his recordings of 139 dead people, among whose voices one can apparently pick out the baritone of Bismarck awaiting reincarnation. Others may require more pungent seasonings, such as, for example, the frog in Liverpool who reportedly crawled out of a shattered block of granite and survived for several hours. A frog in the grass is fine with me.

A Book of Mysteries by Thomas de Jean, three volumes translated by four people, Wydawnictwo Pandora, 1993.

THE VANDALS' FATE

&

WHAT HAVE THE VANDALS bequeathed to popular memory? Only the notion of vandalism as senseless destruction. The author (erudite, and a splendid writer) reminds us that destruction has been a constant in human history from the start, and it's not at all certain that the Vandals rank among its leading practitioners. The tragedy here derives from the fact that their chief enemies knew how to write, whereas the Vandals despised the art of arranging letters to the end of their days. Whatever information we have about the Vandals comes from their enemies and is inevitably less than favorable. You can't expect much by way of subtlety from enemy accounts; they don't enter into the mentality of a troublesome tribe, they don't seek out the reasons behind their acts. Some of the Vandals' decisions bear in our eyes the stamp of collective insanity. I'll give an example. We know that in the first centuries A.D. the Vandals inhabited the southwestern territories of what is now Poland and the banks of the Cisa. Suddenly they abandon these warm settlements and in 406 are spotted by the Rhine. Displaced by stronger rivals? Not necessarily, since over the next decade or so they demonstrate enough force to terrorize Gaul and Spain. And suddenly, once again, they abandon Spain, where they'd settled in pretty comfortably and weren't under threat, to conquer the north shore of Africa. On ships, by sea, that is, out of their native element, in an alien climate and an unknown world... With their women, their children, and whatever plunder they'd picked up over the years. They establish a state in Africa, small and weakly rooted in the reality that surrounds them. A hundred years later Byzantium attacks and defeats them after a brief war. But what happened to the Vandals? They can't all have fallen in battle or perished in captivity. There are always a few survivors and perhaps a mournful song passed from one mouth to the next for a few generations.... Yet the Vandals cease to exist from one day to the next without a trace; they evaporate from history's pages without a word of self-commentary. You don't even hear someone down the line laying claim to a Vandal great-grandmother or at least a nanny. Only in the thirteenth century—red alert, red alert—do the Poles begin to flaunt their Vandal ancestry. There may even be a grain of plausibility in this perception, considering that the Vandals settled on our lands for quite some time. But please, please stay calm. There's no need to leap up in the night with your hair on end and a shriek of horror on your lips. The Polish chroniclers proclaimed our Vandal heritage. Which means that we had chroniclers. Which means, in turn, that we'd already begun to have literature. And this in conclusion demonstrates that this isn't a case of some fatalistic inheritance of traits, among them a ruinous aversion to writing.

The Vandals and Their African State by Jerzy Strzelczyk, Warsaw: Panstwowy Instytut Wydawniczy, 1992.

What's Dreaming?

ഗ

THERE'S A SCENE IN one of Fellini's films where the workers extending a subway line come upon an Etruscan
crypt covered with dazzling paintings. Unfortunately, as soon
as other people rush to the scene, as soon as the photographers take out their cameras, the paintings begin to dim,
fade, turn gray. Finally, after a brief moment, bare walls appear before the eyes of the mute, helpless onlookers....It's
the same thing with dreams: they scatter and vanish irretrievably the moment we wake up. Sometimes, but again briefly,
we retain a strong impression from them. Even more rarely
do we manage to hold onto a single image, a situation. Psy-
choanalysts would say that this is as it should be—the dreams
we don't remember are obviously less important than the
ones we do. I wouldn't be so sure. A lot may depend on the
circumstances surrounding our awakening. But fine, let's say
that the dreams that we're able to recall mean more than the
ones after which we turn over to our other side. The big shots
of psychoanalysis bother me for a different reason. For them,
a dream's a dream, but what they really study are only re-

tellings of dreams, and this makes a difference. In retelling our dreams we use some sort of syntax to organize and rationalize, that is, to modify, their enigmatic chaos. The precision of our narrative will also depend on the vocabulary we command and even on the literary traditions we've absorbed. Every good translator knows how much trouble it is to transpose the various nuances, tones, and accents from one language into another. Should translating dreams into waking speech be easier? Let's suppose that three gentlemen, from China, Saudi Arabia, and Papua New Guinea, all have exactly the same dream one night. I know that it's impossible, but humor me. Upon awakening they would undoubtedly give three very different accounts. Different linguistic systems, different modes of narration, different stockpiles of concepts and associations...So much has been written on the subject of psychoanalysis that it's difficult to imagine that doubts of this kind have never been voiced before. I'll say only that my own very modest reading in this area has yet to turn anything up. Likewise in this book comprised of three very typical essays by Jung, the dreamed dream and the narrated dream are one and the same, without reservations....This puts a slight damper on my uncritical admiration.

On the Nature of Dreams by Carl Gustav Jung, translated by Robert Reszke, Warsaw: Wydawnictwo KR, 1993.

Too Late, or When?

❧

Karel Capek published his famous catastrophic novel in 1936. It was conceived as a warning against the growing power of Hitler's fascism. Hence today we should treat it as a worthy classic, that is, put it on a shelf with other books that were absolutely right in their time—and stop reading it. If we do read it, then only for the sake of its stylistic and conceptual inventiveness. I read *The War* this way, for fun, some twenty years ago. While I was rereading it now, a cold chill ran up my spine time after time, since the book hasn't aged, unfortunately. What's it about? Some people stumble on a small colony inhabited by an unknown species of amphibian on the shores of some distant island. They also accidentally discover that these friendly-looking monsters are fairly quick-witted and can be taught to perform various underwater tasks, that they acclimate readily to all latitudes, and that, when regularly fed and properly equipped, they can provide the human race with countless benefits. This is the introduction. In the epilogue it turns out that the newts have multiplied beyond count and no longer fit inside the little bays to which they've been assigned. As a result they gradually overflow onto all the

continents and sink them into the ocean. Capek fills the
space between the introduction, where nothing looks ominous yet, and the epilogue, in which it's too late for any opposition, with the buzz of information. The novel is a parodic
montage made up of the most varied kinds of communica-
tion. We get news reports, experts' testimony, and statistics.
Interviews, statements, lectures, and polemics. Appeals, procla-
mations, and manifestos. An ever-growing number of rallies,
congresses, briefings, and summit meetings. All on the subject
of the newts, in conjunction with the newts, in opposition to
the newts, and in defense of the newts. It becomes increasingly
clear that there's no possibility of reaching any kind of agreement. As time goes on, moreover, opportunists turn up who
work to provide services to the newts. The ranks of those
who want only peace and quiet, who've had enough of those
damned newts, continue to swell as well. Naturally, there's also
no dearth of foresighted individuals warning and exhorting.
But, good Lord, in the beginning how can you tell a demented naysayer from a prophet with right on his side? The
world is full of all sorts of sleeping powers—but how can
you know in advance which may be safely released and which
should be kept under lock at all costs? Between the moment
when sounding the alarm would be laughably premature and
the moment when it's already too late, a single, suitable, perfectly timed moment must occur when the misfortune can still
be averted. In all the commotion it most often passes unnoticed. But which moment is it? How do we recognize it? This is
probably the most painful question posed to human beings
by our own history. Dear Mr. Capek, Esteemed Otherworldly
Shadow—we still don't have the answer.

The War with the Newts by Karel Capek, translated from the Czech by
Jadwiga Bulakowska, Wydawnictwo Siedmiorog, 1992.

Your Honor

cJlp

SILENT NIGHT... Peaceful night...Night that envelops the whole world in sleep...The naturalist who stumbles upon such phrases smiles in pity. Ah, poets, poets. They glide across a landscape's surface, a momentary mood, a fleeting impression suits them fine....Since night isn't really silent or peaceful anywhere—with the exception of the lands of eternal ice, where there is absolutely nothing to hunt and no one to do the hunting. It envelops only a fraction of all living things in sleep. Of the more than four thousand species of mammals, nearly 70 percent do their hunting at night. To say nothing of the many reptiles, amphibians, insects, and birds who emerge from their diurnal hiding places only after nightfall. Thus nocturnal silence is made up of rustling, growling, splashing, slurping, whirring, rattling, fluttering, chattering, and squeaking, not to mention all the sounds that our ears don't pick up. Various furtive assassinations are carried out to this sound track; their victims include birds and their eggs, frogs and their polliwogs, moths and their larvae, lizards, snails, fish, grasshoppers, crustaceans, all sorts of small mammals, and the offspring of large mammals. In warmer regions, where the predators include boa constrictors, jaguars, and alligators, even large animals aren't safe. Someone will remind me that herbivorous animals also go out scouting for meals at dusk, which slightly softens the image of nighttime as a wholesale slaughterhouse. I see their point, but, in the first place, few species are satisfied with plants alone—the majority will snack on the occasional butterfly or grub while grazing. And, second, the question arises whether vegetarianism is so innocent after all. I may incur the wrath here of persons professing vegetarian principles, but, after all, plants are also organisms endowed with the will to live. In other life forms this may be self-evident, but does that mean it isn't present here? However we define this will, though, the fact remains that it meets its end on the plate of the human herbivore.... What I'm saying isn't pretty, but investigating the nature of Nature generally leads to unpalatable conclusions. We humans also take our nourishment at the cost of others' lives: I consider this a scandal. The scandal is the greater since we must, willy-nilly, participate, which we often do with great relish. But enough complaining; it's time for a joke. Your Honor, cries the lawyer in his plea, my worthy opponent delights in tarring my defendants with all the worst possible failings. Yesterday he accused one citizen of having the unmitigated gall to commit his robbery in broad daylight. Today he accused another guy of shameless underhandedness, since he pulled off his heist at night. So I ask you, Your Honor, just when are my clients supposed to do their stealing?

Nocturnal Animals by Hanna and Antomi Gucwinski, from the series *Animal Mysteries*, Wroclaw: Wydawnictwo Dolnoslaskie, 1993.

Roman Thickets

⁂

IT RARELY OCCURS TO us that all the ancient texts we know derive not from the original versions, but from copies. And chiefly from copies transcribed many times over, at various times and with various intentions. How far can we believe such texts? Even the most scrupulous copyists occasionally omitted or distorted something. Besides, whoever was paying them might demand certain changes, especially if the work concerned a past that nobody remembered. Thus, for example, in the fourth century B.C. Rome held several ambitious families anxious to be descended from the mythological Aeneas, or, as a last resort, from the later but equally mythological Romulus. This is why the copyists took every opportunity to insert these purported progenitors into their texts, naturally ascribing to them various heroic deeds (largely borrowed from other mythologies), or showering them with titles and posts that didn't exist in those distant times. But why talk about the copyists? These families were so wealthy that they even commissioned completely new legends from historians for their own personal glory. And upon occasion to strike a blow at competing families, whose equally falsified forebears took the shape of cowards and traitors. Family concerns were soon joined by state interests. The plan was to draw from the murky thickets of myth and legend a straight, unequivocal road leading the Romans from triumph to triumph. In reality, this road was winding, bumpy, and in some stretches virtually imperceptible. There was, for example, the miserable business of the Roman kings who bore, as if from spite, Etruscan names. There was also the nuisance of those enemies to whom the valiant Romans dealt a "crushing" defeat in every battle. In very short order, though, they were forced to go to battle with the same enemies yet again, and to rout them once more, after which it turned out that the deceased had once again donned armor and discovered mighty allies. Doubts of a moral nature also cropped up. According to the myth, the city of Rome (yet another Etruscan name) was founded by two brothers, Remus and Romulus (Etruscan names again). Unfortunately, Romulus killed his brother, which didn't fit with notions of Roman virtue. Versions glossing over the fact of this fratricide began to circulate. Remus was a scoundrel and earned his death many times over; Remus was a scoundrel, but somebody else killed him; Remus wasn't a scoundrel, and was killed in an accident; Remus wasn't killed at all, he just liked the country better than the city and spent his waning days in a cottage by the woods.... In Michael Grant's book the word "propaganda" turns up only a couple of times, although it could in fact be repeated on every page. The fullest blossoming of this art (of sorts) occurred in the age of Augustus, thanks to several exceptionally gifted writers. The Romans treated their past instrumentally. But were they alone in this? Other ancient mythologies also bear traces of ingenious manipulation. If less is known on this subject, it's only because these legends have yet to meet their Grant. I recommend this book to anyone who likes to think things over now and then.

Roman Myths by Michael Grant, second edition, Warsaw: Panstwowy Institut Wydawniczy, 1993.

BLACK TEARS

⌘

T HIS BOOK IS MEANT in principle for everyone, but it's really just for women. I have yet to meet the man who would spend his time studying a handbook of bon ton. In such matters gentlemen rely entirely upon the ladies and their gentle persuasion. The book contains sensible and, by and large, practical suggestions—practical, that is, as long as you live reasonably well and can occasionally spring for something larger than a bus ticket. But in such guides I always miss the final chapter that would describe life itself, which always takes us by surprise. This chapter might be titled "Don't Overdo It," and would explain that on the road to perfection it's wisest to stop a few steps short of the finish line, since it may turn out that the finish line will be found hanging over a cliff. I'll illustrate by way of a story I once read in a French women's magazine. The magazine posed the following question to unfaithful husbands: "Under what circumstances did you first betray your wife?" I'll tell it in my own words because I can't lay my hands on the original. I am—a certain gentleman confided—the owner of a rather prosperous antique store. My wife is distinguished by great beauty; she tends her looks and accents them expertly. Her clothing is tasteful and appropriate. She instills proper morals in the children, and rears them wholesomely. Thanks to her, everything runs smoothly at home. Everything has its place, which gleams with cleanliness. The home-cooked meals are delicious, calorically balanced, aesthetically presented, and punctual. My wife moreover is prudent and tactful, and thus lands on her feet in any situation. My friends think I've found the ideal spouse. And I shared their opinion—up until the day when a certain girl walked into my shop. She wasn't particularly pretty or attractive, and was dressed in cut-rate, unbecoming rags. Her jacket was missing a button and she had dirty sneakers on her feet. She shyly asked the price of a necklace in the window. It wasn't expensive, but it was too much for her. She was about to leave when suddenly, with a careless gesture, she bumped into a stand holding a costly Chinese vase. The vase shattered into pieces. She looked in horror first at me and then at the shards—then plunked down on the floor and started bawling like a child. I was dumbstruck, but various thoughts kept drifting through my mind. For example, that my wife has never bumped into anything. That I'd never seen her cry. That even were she to burst into tears, she'd certainly never do it on the floor. And her tears would be crystal clear, since she used only the mascara manufactured by the famous firm of X....Overcome with emotion, I knelt beside the girl, embraced her, and wiped the streaks of black tears away with my impeccably white handkerchief....And that's how it all began, the straying antiquarian sighed in his final sentence.

The Art of Life, or an Encyclopedia of Good Form by Lady Perfect, Wydawnicto Elew, 1993.

GRAPHOLOGY ON THE BARRICADES

ぷ

I DON'T KNOW ABOUT Poland, but in the West graphologists have got their hands full. Institutions, businesses, and individuals are calling upon their services in ever-increasing numbers. The author of this book is the president of the Association of German Graphologists and represents them at international conferences. Graphologists advise, adjudicate, resuscitate, and participate. All well and good. I've got nothing against graphologists. If anything bothers me, it's the people seeking their advice. Let's compare the clientele of psychiatrists with the clientele of graphologists. The former hope to illuminate the crannies of their own psyches. The latter generally seek to x-ray another person's character, usually without his knowledge or consent. In a graphologist's waiting room, you'll find ladies with letters from their fiancés in their handbags. The writing specialist will determine who'd make the best match. You'll also see gentlemen whose interest rarely lies with the character of their future wives. Their primary concern is penetrating the psyche of their future business partner. There's nothing surprising about one person wanting to know another person as well as possible. Up to this point, though, the methods used to this end have generally been homegrown, such as, for example, spending a lot of time with the given individual, frequent conversations with him or her, occasional card games (for money, of course), shared outings on sailboats or on mountains. But everybody's in a rush these days. Who's got the time for struggling with sails or spreading sleeping bags beneath the peaks? Intelligent observers are few and far between, in any case, since this requires concentration. Conversation doesn't enter the picture either, since this art is seldom practiced in some circles. Hence the fad for graphology. And this fad will persist as long as people still command the skill of writing by hand.... Various private businesses in the West call upon the knowledge of graphologists in assessing candidates for important positions. They require a handwritten résumé from the candidates, which is then passed on to the graphological experts. And the most impressive letters, diplomas, and certificates will be useless if the graphologist responds: "poor interpersonal skills," "lack of organizational ability," "unreliable." The question remains, though, whether this graphologist has himself been graphologically verified. Since his handwriting might turn up such traits as: "reliance on first impressions," "prejudiced against others," "dogmatic." I'm a skeptic; there's no getting around it. So, to derive some personal benefit from the advice this book contains, I submitted a sample of my own writing for graphological analysis. The results can be summarized in a single sentence: And so, Ladies and Gentlemen, I'm not so great, but I could be worse. Which I've known for a long time anyway.

The Art of Writing, or You and Your Character by Alfons Luke, translated from the German by Krzysztof Uscinski, Wydawnictwo Luna, 1993.

I Was Traveling with the Fairest

⨌

THEY'D FIRST SEEN each other scarcely an hour or two earlier, they'd scarcely exchanged a few words and danced a couple of dances and off they went to bed." On hearing a sentence like this we have no doubt that what's under discussion is modern-day debauchery as opposed to earlier times in which stricter morals prevailed. Stricter, granted, but far more shocking. For centuries on end, in various countries and faiths, physical relations between two total strangers were a norm accepted and blessed by secular and church authorities alike. In Europe, royal marriages only recently ceased to be contracted in this fashion. The newlyweds rarely knew each other personally. The preliminary courtship was conducted through diplomatic channels; the candidates themselves exchanged only portraits and letters. The portraits were invariably flattering, and secretaries wrote the letters. Both parties were frequently in for a shock when they finally came face to face on the wedding day. The arrangements and preparations had gone too far for them to turn back, though. The solemn ceremony was followed by a wedding feast, after which the newlyweds were hustled off to the nuptial bed that same night. Today when two people decide upon a thoughtless and precipitate abbreviation of the physical space between them, they think, at least at that moment, that they're mutually attracted and drawn together by an overwhelming force. Nothing like this entered the picture back then. The couple joined from on high had only to fulfill their marital obligation. Thus the wedding night was dominated by paralyzing fear, aversion, alienation, and often physical revulsion. Not only for the girls. The men had their own hell in the wedding bed. Not all of them, especially at the royal court, were attracted to women. There were also those who couldn't be men on command. Under such circumstances the wedding night took the shape of a brutal rape, which was followed by lifelong resentment and repulsion. Let's also add that pedophilia, in marriage at any rate, was tolerated until the late Middle Ages. Twelve-year-olds found themselves betrothed to balding satyrs. But enough of these horrors...I put my book aside, and since I was reading it in a train, I looked around the compartment. Two fifteen-year-old girls were sitting opposite me. Not bad-looking, but not especially pretty either. But if by some miracle they'd been transported to a medieval court, decked in jewels and draped in satin, they'd have passed for perfect beauties. For in earlier times the absence of defects determined loveliness. My girls had never contracted smallpox or rickets, thus their faces weren't pocked and their legs weren't bowed. Any crossed eyes or crooked teeth had been fixed in childhood. If either had ever broken a leg, she didn't have to spend a lifetime limping....My girls have no idea how lucky they are. Sooner or later they'll marry some Tom or Harry. Their choice will turn out to be apt or disastrous, judicious or rash, born of love or calculation. In any case, though, it will be their own.

In the Beds of Kings by Juliette Benzoni, translated from the French by Janina Palecka, Warsaw: Iskra, 1994.

MUMMIES AND US

✐

I ENJOY VISITING archaeological museums. I've already seen jawbones of every imaginable kind, and a fair number of skulls and tibiae arranged in chronological order. I've seen Egyptian mummies in gorgeous sarcophagi, and Egyptian mummies minus sarcophagi and wrappings; American mummies and mummies from catacombs; and human remains preserved in sand or peat. I hope my Dear Reader doesn't conclude from all this that I have necrophiliac tendencies. I look at these dramatic remains because I've got no reason to avert my eyes. And for one other reason: I've always been fascinated by chance and its unpredictable behavior. Thousands and thousands of generations, veritable Himalayas of bones— all vanished without a trace. And suddenly sometime, somewhere some creature stepped in some sticky mud, the mud petrified, preserving the footprint, and conferences convene over that footprint. Or picture this scene, for example: noble Homo erectus sits down beneath a bush to while away the time by gnawing on a nut. He's just the same as all the others in his horde, but something exceptional happens to him alone: the jaw he moves so diligently ends up in a display case some nine hundred thousand years later. Or a certain Neanderthal, moderately attractive, neither worse nor better than the rest, stands at the edge of his cave and, lost in thought, gazes into the distance, scratching his lice-ridden head. He has no clue—how could he?—that he's scratching an exhibit....In ancient Egypt, at any rate, it would seem that chance wasn't called upon to save anything, since this was a civilization which, like no other before or since, preserved the remains of its dead from destruction. Not so fast. Graves were plundered time after time; mummies were stripped of all they had and were either taken for kindling or ground into a powder that purportedly had healing powers. So once again we're forced to admit that only chance's good graces saved whatever now remains....This album is not for the fainthearted. I'm not a shrinking violet, so I viewed the silently screaming skulls, the long-fingered, blackened palms, the bundles holding infant skeletons, without fear or revulsion. All of this is beautiful in some aggressive and overwrought way....But while I'm on the subject, I'll admit that there are sights that exceed my tolerance. I once visited a wax museum. That macabre facsimile of life, the rosy cheeks, the half-smiles, the eyelashes, the mustaches, the glassy eyes behind your back, all that dolled-up deadness, maudlin and pretentious—now that was frightening. I felt sick and had to go out for some fresh air.

Mummies by James Putnam, photographs by Peter Hayman, translated from the English by Bozena Mierzejewska, Warsaw: Arkada, 1995.

Chips Will Fly

೮⁄೯

THE ASSASSINATION OF public figures in the political sphere is a constant leitmotif in history. The author selects and discusses only a few cases—if he'd wanted to describe each assassination mentioned in every historical source, he'd have ended up with a small library of at least a hundred volumes. There have always been and always will be people who believe that a planned assassination must succeed, that is, bring about the desired effects. Whereas in reality—with a few controversial exceptions—this hardly ever happens. The death of the targeted individual either doesn't change anything or it produces results unforeseen by the assassins. But this subject is a river I don't plan to cross at the moment. I followed another thread while reading: the attendant victims, the victims who lost their lives only because they happened to turn up near the gunfire or within range of the exploding bomb. Assassins may be guided by what are, to their minds, the loftiest intentions, but all this high-mindedness goes to hell, since they know full well—they know in advance—that the designated car also holds at least a chauffeur, the airplane carries a crew, the house contains a household. Thirty people perished in the street attack on Alfonso XIII. The king and the assassination went down in history, but the passersby killed by chance made a onetime appearance in the obituaries. The injured, whose numbers must have been far larger, had to struggle through their scarred and crippled lives in indifferent silence.... It might seem that assassinations must have taken a less bloody turn in earlier times, before the use of firearms and explosives. This was rarely true. Ordinarily both the ruler and his entire family—just in case—fell victim to the attack. Contemporary historians noted this, if at all, only in passing. And they generally failed to comment on the fatalities among the bodyguards and slaves who turned up along the way. When you chop wood, chips will fly, says a true and terrifying proverb. Human chips have never been in short supply.... Nowadays, before our eyes, a new form of assassination is flourishing: the terrorist assassination, expressly directed against random victims. It's harder and harder to get at politicians, since they travel heavily guarded in well-armored cars. But bystanders are a different matter; they cluster in train stations, subways, department stores, bars, waiting rooms, and miscellaneous tall buildings. Easy, unarmed game that doesn't put the hunters' lives at risk. They lay the lethal charge wherever they want, then they follow the updates from some secluded hideaway. The bloodier the carnage, the happier and prouder they'll be. Carl Sifakis's encyclopedia doesn't discuss this new kind of assassination. In it we find only kings, emperors, premiers, ministers, presidents, leaders. The biographies of attendant victims are omitted—since after all they'd be difficult to re-create. On the other hand, nothing stands in the way of compiling another encyclopedia, one dedicated to the victims of modern terrorist assassinations. Some of these victims—crippled, blinded, armless, legless, insensate—are, after all, still living. It would be worth showing how they live. Their misfortune was not that they held some rank, some office, but the apparently meaningless fact that at a given moment they went in somewhere, left somewhere, stopped somewhere, or simply went back to their own house for the night. I think the world stands in urgent need of such an encyclopedia. Done scrupulously and impartially, it would be a worthy contender for the Nobel Peace Prize.

The Encyclopedia of Assassinations by Carl Sifakis, various translators, Warsaw: Real Press, 1994.

MONSTRUM

ॐ

THE ILLUSTRIOUS Jorge Borges once published an encyclopedia of fantastic creatures. I regret to say I haven't
seen it. I only know that it contained classic monsters who
have survived the test of time and achieved international ca-
reers: sirens, medusas, leviathans, and so on. Jan Gondowicz's
book expands this menagery to include the more regional
beings, often already forgotten, that he's tracked down in
fairy tales, travel accounts, and medieval lexicons. He also includes relatively recent inventions of purely literary origin.
This project has been beautifully realized; and Adam Pisarek's
attempt to sort this whole herd into types, groups, categories,
and species is also enchanting. I think both gentlemen must
have had a marvelous time at work. While reading I also
thought, with a touch of regret, that all these horrors, once so
full of magical powers, would nowadays have the proper effect only on very small children. I remember how, long ago, I
used to kiss frogs caught in the garden with fruitless heroism;
and every time I entered a dark room I very seriously ex-
pected some loathsome, heavy thing to leap onto my back

with a hideous squeal. Where are those days? one is tempted to say.... But does that mean that the world of grown-ups holds no monsters? Of course it does, and there's one in particular that, in its numerous editions, has stricken, strikes, and will continue to strike genuine horror in adults. You won't find it in this book because, unfortunately, it isn't a creature of fantasy. On the contrary, it's very real and its sturdy, flesh-and-blood existence outstrips every imaginary dragon, werewolf, or ghost. Whoever's been fortunate enough to avoid a face-to-face encounter can hear it and see it each time he turns on the TV. Sometimes this entity takes the shape of someone's talking head and sometimes of a whole triumphant human figure in snapshots from current wars. I'll try to describe it as Gondowicz describes his good-natured scoundrels, although it will be hard to detect benign features in the likeness sketched below. In their place, though, we find symptoms that make the portrait's subject worth pitying, in spite of everything.... "The person possessed by hatred. Known since time immemorial. He doesn't change; only the methods change that he employs in gaining his end. Moderately ominous when he acts in isolation, which, however, rarely occurs, as he is contagious. He spits. He spreads chaos in the conviction that he is creating order. He likes making pronouncements in the first person plural; this may initially be groundless, but it becomes increasingly justified with persistent repetition. He departs from the truth in the name of some higher order. He is devoid of wit, but God save us from his jokes. He is not curious about the world; in particular he does not wish to know those whom he has singled out as enemies, rightfully considering that this might weaken him. As a rule, he sees his brutal actions as being provoked by others. He doesn't have doubts of his own and doesn't want the doubts of others. He specializes, either individually or, preferably, en masse, in nationalism, anti-Semitism, fundamentalism, class warfare, generational conflict, and various personal phobias, to which he must give public expression. His skull contains a brain, but this doesn't discourage him...."

A Fantastic Zoology—Expanded by Jan Gondowicz, organized by Adam Pisarek, Wydawnictwo Male, 1995.

ELLA

F OR SOME TIME NOW I've been meaning to write a poem
about the magnificent Ella Fitzgerald. Somehow it wouldn't
come. As it turns out, though, everything I wanted to say has
already been noted, examined, and underscored many times
over. But there was something else holding me back subcon-
sciously, and now I understand what it was. I know Ella's
singing only from recordings, I've never heard her live. And I
found out from Stuart Nicholson's book that if you haven't actually seen and heard Ella perform, you don't have a clue:
you don't know her swinging improvisations, the incomparable precision of her singing, and her marvelous freedom in
dealing with the music. Anyone who's had that good fortune
must have felt like Odysseus tied to the mast. With one difference: the sirens who tempted Mr. O. had evil intentions
and bad dispositions, but Ella's singing was guileless. Her
voice always held a kind of innocent girlishness and—this
may be the best definition—goodwill toward her audience.
So even if I've got to admit that recordings can only go so far,
I still know enough to cherish the warmest feelings for Ella.

Her voice reconciles me to life, it cheers me. I can't say the same for any other singer. For me she's just the best, and I doubt that anybody else will come along to change my mind....Five years ago Ella Fitzgerald retired after half a century of singing. During that time she received every possible award and honor. She collaborated with jazz's greatest masters, and her records still sell by the millions. Yet at some point in the sixties some listeners' taste began to change. People started noticing certain limitations in Ella's singing. Not in her voice, which surmounted all obstacles with ease, but in her manner. Take, for instance, Billie Holiday, who poured her heart, soul, and various other organs into her songs. But Ella wasn't histrionic. She always kept a little distance from the text; she never worked the song into a lather. And thank heavens. I see this as yet another leaf for her laurels. Expressive singing is a slippery slope; once you're on it it's hard to get off. We've now reached (I hope) the final phase of this expressiveness. We no longer listen to singing, but to the screeching of strained voices for which any kind of musical finesse is meaningless, and is replaced by bass-boosted decibels. The sentiments may be noble, e.g., all people should be brothers, we should love nature, etc. But the way they're presented is terrorist. "Let's get out of here," as Woody Allen said in one of his films; "when they're done, they'll start taking hostages."

Ella Fitzgerald by Stuart Nicholson, translated from the English by Andrzej Schmidt, Warsaw: Amber, 1995.

Take the Cow

ॐ

HOMEGROWN PSYCHOLOGY depends upon dispensing good advice. Almost all of us traffic in this trade in our dealings with friends and acquaintances. In this we are generally principled and disinterested. But it doesn't ordinarily occur to us to keep a list of our scraps of wisdom and then publish it. It did occur to Mr. Dale Carnegie—and thus we have this guide on how to battle those worries that, needless to say, destroy our health, disturb our sleep, and sabotage our self-esteem. His advice is reasonably well-meaning. It may even help certain people under certain circumstances up to a certain point for a certain period of time. But the author's vocabulary lacks terms such as "perhaps," "partially," "occasionally," and "if." His optimism is unbridled and takes at times an orgiastic shape. This kind of faith instantly whets my skepticism and my suspicion that the absence of all worry would be even worse than worrying. Such an absence betrays insensitivity, lack of imagination, and intellectual crassness. The immediate impetus that prompted the author to write his book was a visit to the public library at the corner of Fifth Avenue and Forty-second Street. He found only twenty-two books in the section under "Worries," whereas there were eighty-nine titles under "Worms"! Unfortunately, though, he was scouting the wrong shelves. If he'd taken a look at the literature section, he would have realized that hundreds of thousands of books have been written about worrying. Virtually all of world literature marks an attempt to cover the entire gamut of worrying—beginning with *Gilgamesh, Antigone,* and *The Book of Job.* I won't keep counting, since this list could go on indefinitely. I'll just suggest a glance at *Hamlet* from this angle. Of course there's the vastly worried hero of the title. All the other characters, not excluding the Ghost, also worry, each for slightly different reasons. Only Fortinbras would seem to be relatively carefree, but let's keep in mind that he turns up only at the last minute and doesn't really unburden himself to us. We can rest assured, though, that as soon as he gets settled on the throne, the troubles will come buzzing around like flies. Of course literature also gives us characters who are entirely worry-free. As a rule though, these are either brainless simpletons or all-knowing father figures still rustling with the paper they're written on. I should by rights leave this how-to book in peace and wish it success at least among those readers who find it easier to keep a straight face. I had trouble with this. Especially while reading "the real-life examples" with which the author seasons his conclusions. For example, some guy was so upset by his wife's illness that he ruined six teeth. He clearly should have cheered up for the sake of his own jaw. Another guy had no luck on the stock market as long as he kept worrying; he made a killing as soon as he stopped. Carnegie sees the cow as a splendid example for wives of straying husbands, since it "doesn't get riled just because the bull takes a shine to another cow." On the whole the examples he gives vividly summon up the reports presented at the Temperance Association in *The Pickwick Papers*. Go ahead and look it up—volume II, section 4. And if you don't keep *The Pickwick Papers* around the house, I don't even want to hear about it.

How to Stop Worrying and Start Living by Dale Carnegie, translated from the English by Pawel Cichawa, Warsaw: Studio Emka, 1995.

WINDFALL

ℐℒ

THERE ARE DIARIES and diaries. The diary Witold Gom-
browicz kept, for example, was conceived with publica-
tion in mind from the start, and thus doesn't cause its author
any posthumous problems. It contains only what the author
had in mind, and it's expressed exactly as he intended. Diaries
meant for private use have it much worse. They're written
without literary cosmetics and self-censorship in order to organize the day just past, to deal with various forms of stress—
and are hidden from even one's nearest and dearest. Thomas
Mann kept such a diary throughout his life. He apparently
managed to destroy part of it, and meant to burn the other
part later, but either forgot or didn't bother. We readers are
now free to inspect his confessions, which is of course connected with the great if ambiguous pleasure of spying and
eavesdropping on someone else's secrets. I remember the
uproar caused by the diaries' appearance in Germany. Everybody scurried to sniff out all the writer's blunders and missteps, his emotional involvements, his snap judgments, his
vacillations, his peevishness, his displays of despotic egotism,

and various other defects. It's difficult to examine your own conscience, but scrutinizing someone else's is painless and always confirms our conviction that we're better. Thus people took full advantage of the windfall offered here. Someone even charged the great writer with a truly disarming crime: T. M.'s own writing concerned him far more than the writing of others.... In the present Polish edition of the *Diaries*, the excellent translator, who also wrote the introduction, likewise could not resist the temptation to draw up a scrupulous account of the writer's failings: how did he fall short as brother, husband, father, friend, colleague, citizen, and representative of the human race? Since the introduction isn't long, all these faults yield by force to the fact of condensation. In the *Diaries* themselves they aren't nearly so tightly packed. It turns out, moreover, that not every harsh judgment of others was dictated by amour propre; not every fear or doubt was the product of a wayward imagination; not every illness was hypochondria; not every tragedy he experienced stemmed from subjective reasons only. And the writer had every intention of fulfilling the obligations placed upon him, although he didn't always manage to do so, and sometimes simply couldn't. I must confess in conclusion, though, that T. M. was certainly no angel. One question still remains: Does anything along the lines of a literature created by angels in fact exist? I personally haven't had the good fortune to find it. All the things in certain books that charm me, amuse me, move me, that make me think or somehow help me in life were produced by very imperfect mortals.

Diaries of Thomas Mann, translated from the German by Irena and Egon Naganowski, vols. I-III, Poznan: Dom Wydawniczy Rebis, 1995.

WILLEM KOLFF

❧

WILLEM KOLFF. Who's that? Some politician or other, a singer, an actor, an international swindler? So many names flurry around us endlessly. They go in one ear and out the other. We've forgotten most of them by the next day. It doesn't bother us. We believe in a just Sieve of Time that sifts the sand until only lumps of gold—the names really worth knowing—remain on the bottom. It's a lovely image, but is it always borne out by reality? I suspect that the Sieve's been punctured here and there, and that the occasional lump of gold slips out with the sand. Willem Kolff is a name still known perhaps to a few specialists, but to no one else, even though it deserves a lasting place in our collective memory. Kolff was a Dutch doctor who invented and constructed the first artificial kidney. This apparatus (granted, still quite cumbersome) remains the only hope for patients waiting for an organ transplant. Kolff couldn't even dream about transplants. He was interested in compensating for ailing, malfunctioning kidneys until they healed (with luck!) and resumed their original function. The conditions under which Kolff performed his initial experiments were rather ghastly. They took place in a small provincial hospital ill-equipped for such fantasies—and all this was during the Nazi occupation. Everything was in short supply: hypodermic needles, which had moreover rusted from repeated use, rubber tubing, and the necessary utensils. Some parts of the machinery had to be ordered from the local cooper; components made of enameled tin were procured illegally from a small factory nearby. Man-made sausage casings stolen from a butcher shop served to filter poisoned blood—that is, the machine's key component. The casings frequently burst, and blood and fluids from the dialysis would flood the floor. The staff would stand for hours on bricks placed beneath their feet, since of course they didn't have waterproof footwear either. The Germans were everywhere, monitoring everything. The argument that in secret operating room number 12A the staff was working for the good of all humanity wouldn't have carried much weight with them. You were supposed to work only for the Third Reich, and anything else smacked of sabotage. Kolff's experiments didn't meet with immediate success, but each following effort prolonged his patients' lives—by a day or two, a week. Victory finally came a year after the war's end: the first patient saved thanks to an artificial kidney. Shortly afterward Kolff and his machine left for the United States, where he continued to improve and modernize it. It's difficult even to calculate how many thousands of people it has saved since then.... Jurgen Thorwald's book is, as its title indicates, about patients, but on occasion he talks, naturally enough, about doctors too. That's how I stumbled onto Willem Kolff, and somehow I couldn't help writing about him. Especially since in our Great World Encyclopedia I couldn't find anything at all on him, not even a couple of lines.

Patients by Jurgen Thorwald, translated from the German by Mieczyslaw Oziemblowski, Krakow: Wydawnictwo Literackie, 1994.

HAMMURABI AND AFTER

ৡ৴

HISTORIANS KNOW A fair amount about Hammurabi, the
ancient Babylonian king who lived more than thirty-
seven hundred years ago and who authored, or, rather, inspired the famous *Code*. We laymen hardly know anything,
only that he's the epitome of an exceptionally harsh and
ruthless lawgiver. Of course, but the ancient laws were never
any gentler back then. And if somewhere they did in fact have
more lenient laws, we'd have to accept this novelty with happy
astonishment. Hammurabi simply had the good luck (and si-
multaneous misfortune) to order that his laws be engraved
on long-lasting stelae made of diorite. One of these was preserved almost in its entirety, and thanks to this he's been stuck
with a reputation for being an unprecedented bully. In addition to a pompous introduction and conclusion, the text of
the *Code* includes 282 paragraphs. I counted thirty-six crimes
punishable by death, and sixteen that called for the permanent crippling of the perpetrator. The remaining offenses
were to be punished by loss of property, exile, or fines of varying amount. As we see, the executioners earned their keep in

Babylon. But we shouldn't let our superiority complex get the best of us. Hangmen still have their hands full in countless countries today. Countless judges pass the highest sentence without worrying their heads over trifles like "presumed innocence," "the right to a defense," "mitigating circumstances."...But back to the *Code*. The reader is struck by a certain rationality—primitive, yes, but present nonetheless. For example, only one paragraph deals with witchcraft. The accused was subjected to trial by water. If he came out alive, his accuser was put to death. Well, it wasn't that long ago that the accuser's complete immunity was the driving force behind all witchcraft trials. The *Code*'s treatment of animals also deserves mention. If a domestic animal killed or maimed someone, only the animal's owner was held responsible for the accident. As late as the Middle Ages, though, we still find grotesque trials and executions of animals. For Hammurabi, at least the animal was innocent, and the human was punished only in the case of negligence. People were also punished for other oversights: untilled fields, uncaulked dams, orchards not fertilized on time. On the other hand, they weren't held responsible for natural disasters, floods, droughts, plagues, and so on. Such calamities befell humans at the gods' behest. Whereas even in our twentieth century, at moments of extreme peril and panic, magic thinking sometimes regains its sway over people, along with the unchecked impulse to assuage their helplessness and despair by way of one scapegoat or another. And now something from Herodotus to wind things up. So we have Xerxes, the Persian ruler who settled on Hammurabi's lands thirteen hundred years later, unfortunately without knowing his *Code*. During his expedition to Hellas, he ordered his forces to throw a bridge across the Hellespont, but the raging sea quickly smashed it. The king was furious and ordered the engineers to be beheaded, while the sea was condemned to flogging and taken into eternal captivity by way of shackles flung into the water. In other words, the people were punished for building the bridge so badly, but the sea was punished for destroying such a splendid bridge.... Hammurabi's logic was of a higher order.

Hammurabi's Code, introduction, commentary, and translation (all very interesting) by Mark Stepien, Warsaw: Alfa, 1996.

DISNEYLAND

♪

THE FIRST TO DISCOVER caves were of course those animals who could find their way in the dark. Cavemen,
who had already lost this gift, couldn't venture too far into
their caves. They had to stick to the edges. It's not that they
didn't have the nerve, they just didn't have flashlights. The
light they had at their disposal consisted of resinous wood
chips and burning oil, both easily extinguished by every passing breeze. With equipment like this, feats such as plunging
into lakes of black water in search of the entrance to the next
grotto or squeezing through narrow underground fissures
were out of the question. Caves have always sparked our curiosity, but this is why the systematic exploration and study of
caves really got underway only in the twentieth century. And
it continues to this day, since there are still more unknown
caves than known ones. Caves that are familiar, accessible,
buttressed against cave-ins, are now tourist meccas. Special
narrow-gauge railways transport the visitors, while the grot-
tos themselves come equipped with various bridges, chairlifts,
handrails, scenic way stations, and so on. And of course spot-
lights are required in order to draw all the splendid shapes

and subtle colors out of the darkness. Required? Well, maybe. But do we really need the lights that have started turning up in some caves? If only their light were neutral, subordinate to what we're supposed to be looking at. Unfortunately this isn't always the case. If the rock is rusty, a colored spotlight makes it even redder. If you stumble upon some delicate celadons, yellows, pinks in the limestone, the spotlight will intensify their tints tenfold. And if the stone is white as snow, then the spotlight gives it a hint of color. Disneyland is invading our caves. Nothing is left in its natural state for our discrimination and perception. Oh, and sometimes you even get a little Muzak. Since of course Disneyland can't tolerate quiet either. Things have to be bright and bouncy. Otherwise natural phenomena might retain their innate dignity....And since I'm on the subject, I'll just mention that Disneyland has also started invading art museums, where ancient sculpture fares the worst. You see statues, torsos, busts to which the spotlight adds a touch of sky-blue, a dash of orange. So that they'll be "even lovelier"...I hope I'm wrong, but I think this is making our eyes dumber.

Caves by David E. Portner, translated by Marek Zybury, Wroclaw: Wydawnictwo Atlas, 1995.

HUGS FOR HUMANITY

❦

THE AUTHOR GIVES the impression of being someone who sincerely believes what she's writing, and she writes that people would be incomparably happier if they spent more time in each other's arms. She has in mind friendly hugs, without any ulterior motives. Well of course, fine, why not...I'm just a little unnerved by her call for the intensification of these hugs in time and space. We all know that a gesture repeated too often grows trite and loses its deeper meaning. In American TV series someone flings himself or herself into someone else's arms every three and a half minutes, which nonetheless doesn't mean that the previous intrigues, grudges, and misunderstandings have all been consigned to oblivion and that a series planned for twenty episodes will expire prematurely. In real life it's no different. We Poles in particular have something to remember here. Never did we hug each other as collectively, eagerly, resoundingly, and avidly as during our Saxon era in the eighteenth century, and somehow nothing good came of it. Kathleen Keating is an American, and enthusiasm comes to her more easily. We find in this little book specific directions as to whom we should hug, where, when, in what way, and what for. But one thing at a time. Whom—obviously, anyone who doesn't struggle; when and where—why, always and everywhere, of course. In the workshop, in the kitchen, in front of the movie theater and in it, in the lecture hall, at committee meetings(!), while running(?) for the bus, picking strawberries(!!), sorting letters at the post office(?!), and even (how on earth did she come up with this one?) while conducting archaeological excavations. In what way—oh, every which way. There are "bear" hugs, "sandwich" hugs, "side-to-side" hugs, "back to front" hugs, and many, many others. And why are we supposed to do all of this? Naturally, to express our democratic and altruistic feelings, and, if we happen to be embracing in the bosom of nature, our ecological feelings as well. Moreover, casting our arms around one another fortifies the nervous system, distracts us from eating (which in turn helps to keep our figures trim), develops the muscles by compelling us to perform various motions, and checks the aging process. Who am I to scoff at such pleasing promises? I confess, though, that I'm relieved at the thought that the author lives a long way off, on the other side of the ocean. If she were my neighbor and happened, moreover, to like gardening, I'd have to sneak secretly out of the house and lie in wait for a moment when Ms. Keating was digging with her back turned to me. Otherwise I'd be unable to escape the requisite attack of affection, and, what's more, I'd be forced to reciprocate. We'd thus be locked in each other's arms several times daily. She undoubtably in hopes of rejuvenating me. And I with an eye to that garden, which—heaven knows—might turn up future excavations?

A Little Book of Hugs by Kathleen Keating, drawings by Mimi Noland, translated from the English by Dariusz Rossowski, Wydawnictwo Ravi, 1995.

Truth and Fiction

❦

Pythagoras, one of the earliest Greek philosophers, is
an almost completely mythologized figure. We know
only that he lived in the sixth century B.C., that he must have
had contact with Eastern thinkers, and that he founded a
school which cited him in all its works. We also know that he
didn't write down his teachings and elaborated his ideas only
in the numerous apocrypha that appeared after his death.
Historians of philosophy thus prefer to speak of Pythagorean
philosophy rather than the philosophy of Pythagoras himself. Some even doubt the authorship of works traditionally
attributed to him....This is probably overdoing it. The master must have been a fairly imposing person with impressive
scholarly credentials in order to found a school and attract
followers. Legends don't totally overgrow just anyone. He set
his school going in two directions at once: it dealt both with
maximally precise sciences (geometry, acoustics, astronomy)
and with virtually unverifiable metaphysical speculations. The
times were such that one didn't hinder the other. "Feeling
and faith speak more forcefully to me than do the wise man's

lense and eye...." The Pythagoreans would be baffled by such formulations. What kind of choice is this? Why do you have to take sides? Even though I'm not a Pythagorean, I'll admit that this Romantic phrase rubs me slightly the wrong way, too. After all, science (that is, the despised "lense and eye") would never have gotten anywhere without imagination, intuition, and an intellectual willingness to tackle mysteries—that is, without everything encompassed by "feeling and faith." Nor can poetry be ascribed exclusively to one side. I can easily imagine an anthology of the most beautiful pieces of world poetry making room for Pythagoras's theorem. And why not? It sets off the sparks that are the mark of great poetry, its form is pared beautifully to only the most necessary words, and it has a grace with which not even every poet has been blessed.... The school Pythagoras created lasted for nearly two centuries, and was thereafter periodically revived in various forms. The master's cult continued to thrive, and his successive biographies accrued ever more copious embellishments. The two last biographies date from the third century A.D.; by this time, they're swimming in miracles. Pythagoras ceases to be an ordinary mortal and is promoted to Apollo's son, then finally turns into Apollo himself, temporarily incarnated in human form. With this kind of pedigree, Pythagoras could at last really cut loose: he conversed with water and with animals, he plucked eagles from the skies who then sat quietly on his hands, he calmed storms, foretold the future, recalled previous incarnations, and even—which must have been tougher than the above-mentioned miracles— called a halt to every tyranny he happened upon in his wanderings. But of course miracles pass and everything goes back to what it was. From Pythagoras we have only (I like that "only"!) his famous theorem. And as a bonus a certain thought expressed under European heavens for the first time: "All living beings are akin to one another."

The Lives of Pythagoras by Porfirius, Iamblichus, Anonynous, translated, with an introduction and commentary, by Janina Gajda-Krynicka, Wydawnictwo Epsilon, 1993.

THE PRINCE'S FEET,
NOT TO MENTION OTHER BODY PARTS

ℐℐℴ

A SURPRISE LIES HIDDEN in this sketch. I won't say where, because then, Gentle Readers, you would go looking for it straight away. So all in good time. The book's subtitle reads as follows: "Bodily Hygiene from the Middle Ages to the Twentieth Century." One should add "in France," since the author draws exclusively on French chronicles, letters, memoirs, and medical tomes in reaching his conclusions. But one suspects that the history of cleanliness would look more or less the same in all the countries of Europe. People in the Middle Ages did bathe occasionally. Public baths sometimes flourished in the larger cities, but they were all eventually shut down in the fifteenth century due to periodic reappearances of the plague. One might naively assume that bathhouse patrons could wash up just as well at home. But people no longer washed at home. According to the theories of the time, water was guilty not just of spreading the plague. It was also to blame for all manner of individual illnesses, which took the shape of miasmas that penetrated the inner organs by way of the defenseless skin. The sixteenth, seventeenth, and even partly the eighteenth centuries were eras of inconceivably dirty people. It's true that newborns were washed right after birth, but they were rubbed down immediately afterward with a paste made of ground molluscs in order to neutralize the bathwater's baneful effects. The feet of the future King Louis XIII were first washed sometime after the young prince's sixth birthday. A certain lady once wrote of Louis's father, Henry IV, that "he stank like rotten meat." Since all the courtiers back then smelled rotten, the King must truly have been exceptionally rank. Cleanliness at that time consisted of wiping one's skin with white kerchiefs and using scents. Water was dabbed only on one's face and hands. And if someone decided to take a bath once every couple of years, this was an event to be discussed at length both in advance and after the fact. The master of the house would step into the tub first, then the lady, then their parents, and after them, the children, from oldest to youngest, would submerge themselves in the same liquid, to be followed finally by the servants. If there were cranks who insisted on bathing more often, they had to conceal this passion so as not to be taken for degenerates or libertines. I sometimes think about those historical films that work so hard to reproduce their era faithfully. The actors promenade in costumes and wigs borrowed from old portraits. The sets and props are beyond reproach. But not a single director has as yet resolved to show the dirt, the eczemas, the fungi and manges, the pustules infected by a barber's filthy fingers, and, last but not least, the lice, which during the course of delightful candlelit suppers must have tumbled time and again into somebody's soup. Such films would finally be beyond endurance. Heroic moments or love scenes would move the modern viewer not to tears, but to vomiting....And at last the promised surprise. So, Ladies and

Gentlemen, the great Michel Montaigne belonged among the ranks of those eccentrics who were not revolted by water. Michel Montaigne bathed! Frequently! Willingly! In spite of the mores of his thoroughly grime-covered age! My pen drops from my hand in astonishment.

Cleanliness and Dirt by Georges Vigarello, translated from the French (sometimes badly), Warsaw: W.A.B. Wydawnictwo, 1996.

THEY WERE

✍

A N UNPLEASANT posthumous adventure befell a certain
seventeenth-century German poet who lived near Düs-
seldorf. His name was Jozef Neumann, but he wrote using the
pseudonym Neander, that is, the Greek equivalent of the ordinary Neumann. When he died, the locals honored him in a
touching fashion: they gave the name Neander to a lovely
karstic valley through which he undoubtedly used to stroll.
But in vain, as it suddenly turned out. Since the middle of the
last century people have associated the valley not with the
kindly poet, but with a piece of a skull discovered there. It belonged to a creature that also took walks in the area—it just
took them several tens of thousands of years earlier. Ever
more frequent and scrupulously monitored excavations confirmed that the creatures, now called Neanderthals, inhabited large expanses of Europe and Western Asia. They even
split into tribes with different cultures and slowly developed
their skills. Initially considered ape-men by anthropologists,
they were at last promoted to the title of Homo sapiens. But
this was an experimental Homo sapiens, an alternate to the

human race that had developed in Africa and was just then beginning to conquer the world, the human race to which we all belong without exception. And science has long linked the extinction of the Neanderthals with us, the newcomers. The peaceful-resolution theory held that the Neanderthals weren't exterminated, they simply blended into the new population. It has been debunked literally within the last few years. Genetic research has proven that crossbreeding was impossible. Another theory has yet to be ruled out, and may never be, though fortunately it has some holes in it. It proclaims that the debut of a new human race in history's arena began with a mass slaughter of the local inhabitants. The terrible word "holocaust" has even been invoked.... But a holocaust involves systematic, purposeful action. Whereas we know that both populations lived side by side for millennia, even occupying the same terrain by turns. The new human race didn't immediately demonstrate its incontestable superiority over the old. There was a time when both fates hung in the balance. It's a fact, though, that the old human race lost out in the end, displaced to ever-poorer hunting grounds. The last Neanderthal skeletons show signs of severe malnutrition. James Shreeve's book is a model of objective, competent popularization. Shreeve visited every accessible excavation site from those times, diligently attended every international conference, followed the raging debates, and knew whom to ask about what while conducting his interviews with specialists. Yet plenty of questions still remain. For example, could the Neanderthal talk? Probably. What sort of social ties did he form? What shaped his spiritual life? His beliefs? His vision of the world? His sense of self? These look like idle speculations, but the book shows that such questions have a scientific basis. I couldn't find one question, though:

Did the Neanderthal cry? Did his tear ducts already respond to pain, and, more important, to a wide variety of woes and miseries? He might not have been able to give them precise names—but would this come as such a shock? I have trouble with that at times myself.

The Neanderthal Enigma by James Shreeve, translated from the English by Karol Sabath, Wydawnictwo Proszynski i Ska, 1998.

Round Dates

✑

In the ninth century, Western Europe lay in a near-fatal collapse. From the south it was plagued by Saracen assaults and conquests, from the north and south by attacking Normans, and from the east by Hungarian invasions. Towns were pillaged and burned, churches were leveled, trade and agriculture came to a halt. Famine and savagery prevailed. Charlemagne's accomplishments survived only in memory. In the tenth century, the situation stabilized somewhat, as people slowly dug themselves out of the rubble. The knightly class began to develop, and along with it, the feudal system, which was certainly a vast improvement on the anarchy that preceded it. And that's precisely the moment when rumors begin to spread about the imminent end of the world as foretold in the Apocalypse.... The year 1000 was to be ushered in by ominous signs announcing the brief but horrific reign of the Antichrist. The old world would then perish, and a new one would take its place as Christ appeared in all his glory. So they had to keep an eye out for these signs. Well, of course, there have always been earthquakes and eclipses of the sun and moon, and calves with two heads are always being born in one cowshed or another. But now these all became omens prophesying final things. Likewise heretics and sectarians, who'd never been in short supply, were suddenly transformed into emissaries of the Antichrist. The year 1000 must thus have passed in overwhelming terror, intense repentance, and outbreaks of panic as people prepared for the worst. So later traditions would have it, at any rate, because, oddly enough, contemporary chroniclers (what few there were) pass over this in silence, even though they record events of the preceding and following years.... The author, a well-known French medievalist, explains this gap very persuasively: since the year didn't live up to the predictions, it seemed silly somehow to write about what actually happened.... This book's appearance is timely. The Second Millennium is upon us and eschatalogical forebodings fill many minds. I don't feel up to drawing comparisons and making analyses. I know only that modern people still retain their ancient fondness for round dates. They think that something old should end and something new should begin. Three letters drawn from my recent correspondence confirm this. The first informed me completely disinterestedly that the end of the world was upon us and would finally call a halt to the silly pastimes on which I had apparently frittered away my entire life. The second letter (actually a thick package) held descriptions of revelations that the sender had recently experienced. He presented himself as a simple man who had trouble writing, which was why he demanded that I fix all his orthographic and stylistic errors and return the corrected text immediately. The third letter informed me that the end of the world was a capital expenditure. Accordingly, the author, who was busy announcing this unpleasant news, provided me with his earthly bank account number and specified the necessary sum. Other letters are en route.

The Year One Thousand by Georges Duby, translated from the French by Malgorzata Malewicz, Wydawnictwo Volumen, 1997.

THE FEMALE PHARAOH

ৠ

LONG AGO — NOT LONG AGO…It depends on who's talk-ing and what they have in mind. For an astronomer, "long ago" means something different from what it means to an anthropologist, and something else again for someone who's trying to summon up the Second World War. If he ex-perienced it firsthand, the war won't be long ago at all. If he was born after it, it will seem like ancient history. Chronology is not always obeyed when it comes to such feelings. As far as I'm concerned, medieval historians seem more remote than the historians of the Roman Empire. The Polish chronicler Wincenty Kadlubek is certainly older than Tacitus. But back to business. Queen Hatshepsut governed Egypt three thou-sand years ago. As the pharaoh's widow she was supposed only to look after his small son from a previous marriage. She soon decided otherwise and proclaimed herself pharaoh — undoubtedly with the support of one court cabal or another. But a female pharaoh was absolutely unthinkable in the Egypt of those times. So she had to change her sex for public purposes and wear a tacked-on beard and man's miniskirt everywhere outside the bedroom. Just imagine if the Queen of England had to glue on a mustache and flop around in size-twelve shoes to give her annual speech in Parliament....It's clear how far we've come since such masquerades and we rightly consider that what went on three thousand years ago happened very long ago indeed. Yet we won't see another episode from the same period that way. It's as if it happened yesterday. Soon after Hatshepsut's death (whether natural or hastened is unknown) they energetically set about erasing her name from the list of pharaohs. Every cartouche bearing her name, every likeness of her as pharaoh, every written reference to her was destroyed. We know this sort of thing very well from other sources. Through large stretches of our twentieth century undesirable political personages were likewise forced to vanish from public memory from one day to the next. Their names disappeared from newspapers and encyclopedias, and palm trees suddenly sprouted over their pictures in group photographs. I suspect, moreover, that this will continue to occur here and there. Trimming history to fit present needs is an iron rule of all satraps. Fortunately they seldom succeed. In Hatshepsut's case odds and ends were overlooked. Now she's back on the list of pharaohs, and Egyptologists today argue only about whether she was really an effective ruler and, if so, what her achievements were. She definitely had one to her credit (if you can count as an achievement not killing somebody you could have killed): her stepson survived and had apparently been fairly well groomed to become pharaoh.

Hatshepsut: The Female Pharaoh by Joyce Tyldesley, translated from the English by Ewa Witecka, Wydawnictwo Alfa, 1999.

Cat Music

♪♪

It's a well-known fact: in order to follow doctor's orders, you have to be healthy as a horse. Most undetected diseases aren't spotted due to an aversion to medical exams and exhausting therapies. But these are nothing compared to treatments employed in other ages. I won't mock here the contents of pills swallowed or operations performed with dirty fingers and no anesthesia. Ultimately we still know very little about disease today. But that's not even the worst of it. The worst thing is that for long ages no one wanted to know more. The entire seventeenth century and nearly three-quarters of the next century were a period of intellectual stagnation as far as medicine goes. People relied on the authority of the ancients: if it wasn't in their books, it simply didn't exist. And since there was nothing about the circulation of the blood, discovered by Harvey, and nothing about vaccinations against smallpox, which Jenner had already begun to administer, official medicine refused to acknowledge these novelties for entire decades. Religious superstitions reinforced this resistance. I read somewhere that, stricken with malaria, Cromwell stubbornly refused to take cinchona bark, whose febrifugal properties were already known. He had a single reason: the medication had reached England under the name of "the Jesuits' powder."...And how did things look in France? Admittedly, France had already managed to produce a Molière, but the mentality of its doctors was not altered by this feat. French archives have turned up a genuine rarity: Louis XIV's "Health Diary," kept by his successive personal physicians. For over sixty years they systematically recorded the royal complaints and their method of treatment. The reader's hair stands on end. During the period under consideration, His Majesty underwent more than two thousand enemas. In between enemas various emetics were employed. In addition, his blood was energetically let, even when he felt fine, "as a precautionary measure," in order to purge the organism....Then, of course, one had to treat the consequences of this treatment, and, subsequently, the consequences of treating the consequences. The King must have been an exceptionally sturdy specimen, genetically programmed to live some 120 years or so, since even when subjected to such methods he survived to almost eighty. His subjects died younger. The average life expectancy was twenty-eight. When a young couple married, usually only one of their four parents was still living. And every fourth child died within its first twelve months. Nonetheless things were improving slightly. Hospitals were ordered to place no more than two invalids in one bed, not three or four as formerly. It's also gratifying to note that mentally ill patients were no longer kept in cages. They were crammed into halls specially designated for that purpose, the raving lunatics, alas, alongside the melancholics. Doctors who actually cared about their well-being did turn up from time to time. In the wealthier hospitals so-called cat pianos even appeared. Live cats took the place of strings—at every touch of the keyboard the creatures meowed piteously. Apparently this provoked the desired merriment among the auditors in that hell.

Early Medical Practice: Doctors, Saints and Wizards of the Seventeenth and Eighteenth Centuries by François Lebrun, translated from the French by Zofia Podgorska-Klawa, Wydawnictwo Volumen, 1997.

THE END OF THE WORLD IN PLURAL

ঙ্গ৴৹

S O ONCE AGAIN the promised end of the world hasn't
come. However, no one is expressing regrets to the esteemed and valued General Public and tickets will not be
refunded. In any case, all the ends of the world that have
actually taken place thus far on earth have arrived unan-
nounced. For example, the end of the world for the great
reptiles occurred some seventy million years ago. Both earlier
and later such animals were decimated by still other ends of
the world. The plesiosaurs had already perished, let's say
about 100 million years ago. One might think that earthly
and cosmic powers had decided specifically to persecute over-
weight reptiles. Nothing of the sort. Scrawny creatures of
unprepossessing proportions also died out as the result of a
wide variety of geoclimactic disasters. Paleontologists recognize
sixteen orders of reptiles; it's enough to note that only four of
these have survived to the present day. Those that were irretrievably lost weren't lost in isolation; they perished alongside
various primeval amphibians, plants, insects, not to mention
archaic fishes and countless other forms of aquatic life. I have

a book about fossils at home—it's like reading one big collective obituary. All those graptolites, blastoids, merostomata, trilobites, belemnites, ammonites, conulata, and tabulata met their end if not in the Cambrian period, then in the Ordovician, if not in the Silurian, then in the Devonian, if not in the Carboniferous, then in the Permian, and if in the Jurassic period, then either in the high, middle, or low Jurassic. Likewise in the Tertiary and Quaternary periods nature had her hands full, and enthusiastically destroyed what she had enthusiastically created earlier. Near the end of the Quaternary we appeared, that is, the people busy building civilization. And we hadn't even taken a good look around when we found ourselves eagerly assisting in nature's more destructive labors. But that's another story, better suited to some dreary December day. Meanwhile, though, it's still summer, the weather's great, and the writer of these words is vacationing in the country and returns as we speak from wandering through the meadows. A tiny lizard suns itself on the steps to my house. Before I can even get a good look at it, it catches sight of me and, with a lightning-quick, astonishingly agile leap, sails into the deep grass. Too bad—I wanted to ask it how it managed to escape unscathed from all those ends of the world, especially the ones that seemed to be directed specifically against it and its relatives. I know I wouldn't have gotten an answer. This wouldn't have kept me from asking other questions. Of course, if it had been an adder, not a lizard, I would have asked them from a safe distance.

Fossils by Karl Beurlen and Gerhard Lichter, translated and adapted by Jozef Kazimierczak, Wydawnictwo GeoCenter, 1997.

THE NUT AND THE GILDED SHELL

ॐ

THE GREAT SINGERS were always stars. Even back before that term was invented. Their admirers rarely allowed their feet to touch the ground, though they did occasionally drop down with a thud. Their fans included not only genuine connoisseurs of vocal art, but also the far more numerous throngs of snobs who clapped, shrieked, hissed, and fainted just because everybody else was doing it. The appearances of Domingo, Pavarotti, and Carreras show that nothing has changed—except that the mass media have upped the decibel level a thousandfold. As concerns gossip and sensational goings-on, Ms. Lewis's book slakes our curiosity completely. It's got everything: spectacular successes, brawls, scandals, backstage intrigues, and affairs. There are also a fair number of photos—one princess or another, several million at a champagne reception, what looks like the latest lover. This is called their "private life," but it's really only the thin layer of gilt that hides the life. Beneath it lies the hard, gray nut, that is, dreary, dogged, persistent drudgery. The author rarely

mentions this. It's boring, unglamorous, and who cares anyway. The obligatory daily breathing exercises and vocal practice, rehearsals with accompanists, rehearsals with partners,
rehearsals with the orchestra, meetings with managers, recordings repeated ad nauseam until you get it right, costume
fittings, interviews during which your guard never drops...
And more hotels, each so much like the previous hundred
that you're finally not sure just exactly where you are. I'm not
convinced that one can be an effective playboy under these
circumstances. The handsome young Domingo spent nearly
twelve months in Tel Aviv, during which he made more than
two hundred appearances and learned more than fifty roles
by heart. If this grind ever permitted the occasional chink of
free time, I doubt that busty supermodels bursting with sili-
cone could squeeze into it. After a performance you have to
get a good night's rest, since you've got another show two
days from now and a new opera to rehearse the next morning. So rumors concerning the amorous conquests of these
otherwise intriguing gentlemen should be cut in half. If not
three-quarters...There are two other troubles that famous
singers can never shake off. First there's the stage fright, far
worse than for actors in the "speaking" theater. No one even
notices if they've got a little cold. But with singers everyone
hears it right off; it becomes the first sign of a fading career.
Singers flash radiant smiles for the cameras, but they're shak-
ing inside, like a weight lifter just before he strides up to the
dumbbells. The second pressure is the endless debate in the
press: which one is the "tenorissimo," better than the other
two?...I think they all sing beautifully, all three are the best,
and I'm equally grateful to all of them. If Pavarotti touches
me a tiny bit more, it's only because he looks like a large

black May bug in his dress coat, and I'm partial to the charm of May bugs.

The Private Lives of the Three Tenors by Marcia Lewis, translated from the English by Bozena Stoklowy, Wydawnictwo Swiat Ksiazki, 1999.

LET ME TAKE THIS OCCASION

ঞ

I WAS STRUCK BY this book's title, and by it's having been a
best-seller in the United States a few years back. In the
States, that is, a country where smokers are now virtually
second-class citizens, since there's nowhere they can smoke—
at work, no, in public places, no, in designated areas, no,
since they don't exist. Maybe at home, but that's a minefield
too, since a spouse who smokes is a legitimate reason for divorce and large alimony checks. Someone who's up for a job
and is photographed in the act of smoking drops out of the
running immediately in spite of his qualifications.... The author is, I believe, a literary scholar. He tracks down texts on
tobacco-smoking that have emerged from the pens of various
famous authors. But his discussions are boring and psy-
choanalytic ad absurdum. I have doubts about the "best-
sellerability" of this book, and admit with distress that I didn't
get all the way through it. I see at the same time that I now
have the space and opportunity to say a few words about this
habit from my own experience. There will be one confession
and two requests. First the confession: I smoke, and I've done

it for years. I regret it, because it's a habit and thus a partial loss of personal freedom. When I'm at someone's house, I ask for permission to smoke, and if anyone present sighs deeply at that moment, I retreat without oaths or reproaches to another room, or to the toilet, stairwell, or garden. As a reasonably mature person I know that cigarettes are harmful to your health. The warnings on the packages don't come as news to me. Yet even assuming that only smokers die of heart attacks and tumors (which isn't true), nature still has a thousand other equally nasty notions on how to remove us from this planet. It may allow nonsmokers to linger a little longer—but that's all that can be said on the subject....And now a request: Dear Nonsmokers! In your passion to persuade, warn, and prohibit, do not mention the nicotine habit in the same breath as alcoholism and drug addiction. This is demagoguery. I have yet to hear of anyone plowing down pedestrians on the highway or routinely slaughtering wife and children while under the influence of tobacco. Moreover, drug addiction consists of flights from reality, whereas smokers, like nonsmokers, labor to create this reality. Sometimes for better, sometimes for worse, but this depends on their talents, opportunities, and temperaments, and not on whether they smoke at work. And the second request: if a black sheep, i.e., a smoker, turns up in your midst, don't create a scene that lasts all evening, and don't make this the only topic of conversation with the smoker. Smoking, after all, is not his principal feature. He has in addition a profession, opinions, passions, experience, and observations, and came to see you not only because you are addiction-free, but also presumably for other reasons. I'm afraid that it may soon come to this: that if someone shows up at one of your gatherings who has—let us say—walked naked to the North Pole and made it back without frostbite, but then carelessly bares himself before you in far worse fashion by reaching for a cigarette, your watchful eyes will register only this last gesture. And the questions will rain down without end: why does he smoke, when did he start, has he tried quitting, why couldn't he keep it up? What a shame.

Cigarettes Are Sublime by Richard Klein, translated from the English by Jacek Spolny, Czytelnik, 1998.

A Word on Nakedness

જી&

ANIMALS DON'T EVEN try to look any different from what nature intended. They humbly wear their shells, scales, spines, plumes, pelts, and down. Even the changes that affect their appearance in certain situations and seasons of life take place automatically. The wolf in sheep's clothing is a figure who frolics in the realm of allegory. This would never occur to a real wolf. The conscious impulse to change one's appearance is found only among humans. In any case we have yet to stumble upon a culture so primitive about which we could categorically state that its creators remain in their natural nakedness. They've always tried to change something, to add something. Please observe that the so-called Willendorf Venus is also not entirely naked. Admittedly she does not wear necklaces or bracelets, but her hair is very beautifully coiffed. And a hairstyle is also clothing. For the author of this book, clothing is primarily fur, fabric, and other materials serving to cover the body. I would also add tattoos, incisions, braids, feathers, and multicolored body painting. All of this clearly means something, signals something. Regardless, it's clothing, not nakedness. Missionaries returning from newly discovered lands described with horror the nakedness of savage tribes. But none of them had actually seen a truly naked person, with the possible exception of newborn infants. Even that's doubtful. Newborns were provided as quickly as possible with amulets against evil powers and the tokens of their tribe. Making a large leap to our own times (the flea should figure on the essayist's coat-of-arms), let's turn our thoughts to what nakedness looks like among us. Naturally, it occurs under many circumstances, but this is only nakedness temporarily undressed for one reason or another. At a nudist beach, you are naked, let's say, from 6:30 A.M. to 7:00 P.M. And that's only in good weather. I once had a chance to take a look at such a beach. And? I didn't see a single absolutely naked person. I saw hats screening faces from the sun, I saw glasses with elaborate frames and feet in all kinds of sandals. Some nudists had watches on their wrists. Since you have to know, after all, when it's time to get back in your regular jeans.

A *History of Clothing* by Maguelonne Toussaint-Samat, translated from the French by Krystyna Szezynska-Mackowiak, Wydawnictwo W.A.B, 1998.

IN RELAXATION'S CLUTCHES

ↄ℘

THERE IS A VAST difference between rest and relaxation. A person who's resting does whatever he wants: if he feels like sleeping, he sleeps; if he wants to walk in the woods, he takes a walk; if he's in the mood for Joyce, he reads Joyce. Such license is impermissible while relaxing. Every moment free from professional labor and other duties should be enthusiastically used for exercise and massage, and to advance preparation of the suitable conditions for exercise and massage. Ladies and gentlemen, no improvising please. Not even mentally, since the mind must also submit to a massage of sorts. Because the goal of relaxation is to get us to the point where nothing bothers us. The ideal promulgated by this kind of popular how-to book is simply a healthy, well-rested idiot. His only object of interest should be his own body. Naturally he requires a few snippets of information about the outside world, which the editors (apparently "experts") are careful to provide. Thus: "the dog is a faithful companion," "natural light illuminates a room," "arrange your furniture so it doesn't get in your way," "enjoy nature's beauty," "dispose of broken items." Fair enough, but why translate all this from English? Wouldn't our native energies suffice to achieve insights like the following: "while breathing we conduct air into the lungs"? And did we need to import from the land of Newton the information that the brain is made up of two hemispheres, of which the left is responsible "for tasks requiring thought, such as the solving of crossword puzzles"? It's not that I have anything against crossword puzzles, but it's typical that these are the only examples of mental exertion. During relaxation, music is of course permissible. It's got to be calm and subdued, though, a pleasing backdrop for knee bends. Whims, however, such as visiting art galleries, attending lectures, going to the theater, or talking to somebody who doesn't mention calorie consumption, are passed over in silence. Books are twice recommended for relaxation, both times as a necessary evil. When your eyes don't droop at bedtime, "try reading a soothing book until you feel sleepy." And when packing your suitcase, "take a book to avoid boredom during a long trip." Finally a personal confession. I love resting. Maybe even too much. Whereas I have never practiced relaxation. I didn't even have a clue as to what I was missing. Now at least I know.

Relaxation: 101 Words of Wisdom, translated from the English, Wydawnictwo Ksiazka i Wiedza, 1998.

MANY QUESTIONS

✑

CAN SOMEBODY WHO wrote eighty fantasy-adventure novels (after starting to write only at the age of thirty-five);
somebody who created hundreds of characters of which perhaps several dozen were endowed with distinct personalities
and two were successfully placed upon the Olympus of literary mythology (I have in mind the enigmatic Captain Nemo
and the enchanting Phileas Fogg); somebody who spent
every free moment reading piles of travel accounts and who
followed all the most recent technological innovations—well,
can somebody like that also find time to nurture his personal feelings, sympathy, friendship, love? Jules Verne's biog-
rapher does not answer this in the positive. To put it bluntly,
Verne, in his monstrous busyness, was a repulsive individual,
a ruthless egotist, a domestic tyrant, perhaps even an emotional cripple. When he died, several generations of readers
mourned him the world over. Whereas in Amiens, where he
lived, not a single honest tear was shed. His family breathed a
sigh of relief, while the inhabitants of that otherwise prosperous town were in no hurry to fund even a modest monument.
His correspondence doesn't speak well for him. He wrote re-

spectfully to his father, but one can't help suspecting that his respect was directed less at the man than at his wallet. His letters to his mother seem more disinterested. He confides in her—about what? youthful longings? love's first stirrings? Not a chance. He regales this elegant lady with accounts of his nagging gastric problems and picturesque descriptions of his stools. When the time came for him to "fall in love" and get married, the one quality of his bride-to-be that merited discussion was her dowry. His letters to his brother display perhaps the greatest human warmth. Unfortunately the final letter, a response to the death of this brother—the closest companion, after all, of his early years—ruins the impression. Only the first two sentences of his condolences to his orphaned nephew express sorrow on his loss. The rest is taken up with complaints about his own failing health, which was not particularly tactful under the circumstances. But the writer's relations with his own son come off the worst. His offspring obviously wasn't to his taste. Verne kept him at arm's length as much as possible. Finally he had the fifteen-year-old placed, through his own efforts, in a ghastly reformatory, and then a year later packed him off by force, like a galley slave, on a ship sailing to the far ends of the earth. It's still not known precisely what the poor boy did wrong. If indeed he did anything, since the main cause regardless was his father, who simply should never have been anybody's father...Uggh!... Hasn't this investigation gone on long enough? And does it really explain anything? Such as how on earth this cold-hearted wretch managed to move and amuse his readers in his books? Or by what miracle this die-hard conservative (not to mention chauvinist) became the bard of unflagging human invention and depicted—beautifully—friendships between the members of the most varied nations? Well, and finally how did it happen that this sinister parent became the most popular, best-loved author of children's books in his time? As we see, you can investigate all you want, but a mystery's still a mystery.

Jules Verne by Herbert R. Lottman, translated from the French by Jacek Giszczak, PIW, 1999.

THE PIANO AND THE RHINOCEROS

♪

THE BOUNDARY BETWEEN health and mental illness is hazy
and follows a different course in every age. Not just psychiatrists, but historians find it difficult to demarcate. We
know, of course, what mental illnesses look like in their most
extreme form. But we also know that there are intermediate
states of varied intensity, and these are more difficult to diag-
nose. Where do you start? First you'd have to define what
mental health is and if in general people do occur who are
completely "normal" from this point of view. I doubt it.
It must be added, though, that their deviations very rarely
end in obvious madness. One may speak only of professional
groups at higher risk. There are two such groups: artists and
rulers. If, however, the dementia of artists may at times occasion masterpieces, the madness of rulers yields nothing but
crises and misfortune. I'm even sorry for a few of these lunatic kings. They might have achieved some sort of equilibrium if they'd changed their workplace in time. For example
England's Henry VI. Affairs of state terrified him. He fell into
long periods of torpor; he'd forget who he was, where he was,

and nothing could get through to him. If he'd just owned a vegetable patch, he might have been happier, both he and his people.... I'm also sorry for Ludwig II of Bavaria, who had no knack for ruling. He preferred the world of his own very costly illusions and sank into it ever more deeply. If he'd been born into some moderately well-off family, he might have become an architect specializing in pretentious palaces for industrialists who listened to music in his spare time. To make things even stranger, when Ludwig drowned in a lake under suspicious circumstances, his brother, who had long since been in less than full possession of his faculties, was dragged onto the throne.... For centuries no one worried about the hereditary transmission of mental illness. All the great dynasties were interrelated; marriages between first cousins were routine. Uncles married their nieces, and their offspring in turn did the same. The grandfather of the above-mentioned Henry was a textbook schizophrenic, while the aunt of the above-mentioned Ludwig was an individual who believed she had swallowed a piano. I should also mention Don Carlos, an unfortunate victim of dynastic hybridization. Schiller later immortalized him as a handsome, freedom-loving prince. In reality, the Spanish heir apparent was a physical and mental degenerate, a raving lunatic and a sadist who liked to watch naked girls being whipped with birch rods, and who personally pushed anyone who irritated him into the next world, preferably by way of the window. When the cobbler brought shoes that were too tight, he forced him to eat them. If he'd managed to ascend the throne, it's doubtful that he would suddenly have become a prudent ruler. But hereditary madness is still not as calamitous as infectious madness. This is what humanity has been up against in our twentieth century, in Europe, Asia, Africa. Its bearers were not kings, but dictators—and dictatorial power creates exceptionally favorable conditions for breeding insanity, which spreads from dictators to entire nations. The best description of this epidemic is probably in Ionesco's *Rhinoceros*. It's too bad this play is produced so rarely, and when it is, it's not done in the places that most need it.

The Madness of Kings by Vivien Green, translated from the English by Tomasz Lem, Wydawnictwo Literackie, 2000.

LACE HANKIES

✧

FOR ME, "MELODRAMA" is not a neutral term, in the way that, say, "Western," "horror movie," "detective movie," and so on, would be. Already toward the end of the nineteenth century people had begun to give this name to romantic dramas of dubious artistic value calculated to move an undemanding public. And I still use the word in this sense today. Maybe I'm behind the times, along with a few other people. The author doesn't make such distinctions and calls every movie about love a melodrama, whether it's trash or a masterpiece. It's difficult to force your own feelings down somebody else's throat, so I'll have to go along with her. Still, I wish that the author, in her introduction to the hundred films she's selected and summarized, had clearly stated that, for example, David Lean's *A Brief Encounter* of 1945 has nothing in common with miscellaneous *Blond Venuses*, and *Out of Africa* is genetically antithetical to, for example, *The Leper*. I'd also have preferred to put the films in chronological order. Something interesting might have come of that. Alphabetical order, though, gets us nowhere. But does this all mean I don't

like melodramas? Not at all. I love them, and the older the
cinematic classic is, the more I like it. It's just that what moves
and interests me isn't exactly what the bygone screenwriters,
directors, and actors had in mind. I'm touched by seeing
beautiful people who are long dead, but still slightly alive.
They dance waltzes gazing deep into each other's eyes, run
through meadows strewn with flowers. And will do so until
the last print has vanished.... The plot doesn't particularly interest me, but I'm taken with the unchanging details. The
heroine always goes to sleep in full makeup and wakes up un-
smudged the next morning. Her day is filled with activities:
she reads notes and arranges flowers in vases. But when it
comes time for a serious tête-à-tête with her husband or lover,
she always sits in front of a mirror brushing her hair. All
is well if the first kiss comes at the end. If the movie begins
with a kiss, woe will follow. Just then, with the regularity of
a cuckoo in an antique clock, someone will pop up who
strongly objects to that kiss. When the woman informs her
beloved that he will become a father, the man receives the
news with unprecedented astonishment, as if realizing for the
first time where children come from. The heroine is sometimes cast into poverty and staggers with hunger—but not for
the world would she be caught staggering in the same dress
two days running. Still, alas, at times she falls ill and dies.
Melodramas consider tuberculosis the most becoming form
of illness. The beautiful stars thus give the impression of
dying in the bloom of health. The men are ordinarily spared
organic diseases. They are most often borne to a palace or
cottage with stabs or gunshot wounds. At this point their
beloved wipes the sweat from their brow with an angelic
smile. Other therapeutic measures are not administered in
melodramas. And oh, those anonymous letters. Anonymous

letters must be believed immediately and unconditionally, and explanations should be withheld as long as possible. Otherwise the movie would end too quickly and the audience would have to return home prematurely. And in real life, as in melodramas, premature arrivals may spell trouble.

One Hundred Melodramas by Grazyna Stachowna, Wydawnictwo Rabid, 2000.

Mountain Climbing

☙

I'M A MATHEMATICAL blockhead—so why did I reach for a book whose plot consists chiefly of what are to me incomprehensible formulas, graphs, and tables? There are two reasons. First, because these enigmatic speculations have their heroes and it's worth reading something about their fates. The main hero is of course the eponymous Pierre de Fermat, a French mathematician of the seventeenth century, the author of several pioneering works. But hardly anyone would remember these if his fame had not been secured by a theorem discovered among his notes. They also suggested that he'd proven his theorem. Unfortunately, no records have been discovered. It's considered almost certain now that Fermat never managed to solve this problem. Mathematics still had to take several dozen baby steps and a few giant steps. The journey was arduous and lasted over three and a half centuries. Every kind of human drama was played out along the way: premature triumphs, dashed hopes, miscellaneous rivalries, not always above board. It even caused one suicide and one duel. But it also prompted splendid collegial teamwork, disinterested

cooperation, spectacular ingenuity, and admirable persever-
ance. The ablest minds grappled with this conundrum. Only
the brilliant Gauss gave up after two weeks. He soon realized
that the proof of this theorem required methods that were as
yet unknown, and if he personally wanted to think them
up and check them, he'd have to live another two hundred
years and drop everything else. As it was, he had a pretty long
life, seventy-eight years, of which seventy-five were spent in
the service of mathematics. No, that's not a typo—Gauss entered the kingdom of numbers as a shockingly bright lad of
three....And the second reason why I bought this book: A
few months ago I watched a program on the Planet Channel,
where I saw with my own eyes an Englishman named Andrew
Viles, who finally solved the problem in 1995. All told he
spent eight years working on it, seven of them in secret. When
he realized that he'd succeeded, he sent off his findings to all
the leading centers of mathematics. Unfortunately, a minor
oversight was discovered and the entire construct crumbled
like a house of cards....Anyone else would have given up in
despair, but not Professor Viles. He worked for another year
with maniacal persistence and in total isolation from the
cares of this world. And lo and behold, this time in a sudden
flash of inspiration he could cry out: Eureka! I watched him
in fascination. Despite his forty years he looked like a schoolboy who, when called to the blackboard, isn't entirely sure if
two plus two equals four. They didn't show his wife, but she's
certainly the one who'd tied his necktie and shoelaces for
him. She's undoubtedly a person who's made her peace with
the facts. Who knows that if she left home for even one day
that her husband would be calling friends for tips on how to
boil the water for his tea and which pots are used for what....
If I've inspired anyone to read this book, I request only that

the reader not ask what was the point of these centuries of mountain-climbing. You don't ask mathematicians and mountain climbers questions like that.

Fermat's Last Theorem by Amir D. Aczel, translated from the English by Pawel Strzelecki, Wydawnictwo Proszynski and S-ka, 1998.

BALLOONS

&

COMIC STRIPS HOLD no special place in my heart, probably because they weren't widely read in my childhood.
I was thus condemned to the arduous and time-consuming
reading of books. I bore this affliction without complaint and
even without feeling that I'd been deprived of something.
And this is still the case today. Later, of course, one comic
strip or another would catch my eye, but only two made any
real impression. I'll get back to them later, though. But now a
few words about Jerzy Szylak's book. He's apparently the first
person in Poland to do scholarly work on comics. He presents
them, rightly, as a significant phenomenon in mass culture, a
phenomenon, moreover, with a fairly rich history and even
prehistory. It's too bad, though, that he stops at the nineteenth century and doesn't delve into time's deeper reaches.
Since what was picture-writing, after all, but comic strips still
on all fours? And later—what about churches, with their series of sculptures and paintings depicting biblical events in
chronological order? Fine, though, let's start with the nineteenth century and its picture books, from which our comics
directly descend. But they're not identical. True comic strips

could arise only after little balloons had appeared and the captions under the pictures had either vanished entirely or been radically curtailed. Investigators have yet to determine where, when, and by whom the little balloons were invented. In any case, these balloons were the deciding factor in the distinctive poetics of comics. And so, for example, the original version of "A Visit from Saint Nicholas" is not yet a comic book. There is a rhymed text under each picture, but when you print the verses separately, the action remains comprehensible. In a comic book, on the other hand, the story line would look something like: "Whiz! Pow! Boom! Bam! Arrggh! Yikes! Ow! Eeeeekkk...Aaaaaaahh!!!!" And in conclusion a single full-blown sentence: "Boss, I'm here to report: mission accomplished."

Now I can turn to my two favorite comics. One came from the pen of Andrzej Mleczko; I used to buy the journal *Pinpricks* every week just for his strip "The Orderly." I came upon the second even earlier. A sweet old shoemaker ran a thriving business near the building I used to live in. He did minor repairs, soles, patches, heels, and sometimes stretched shoes that pinched on a special last. He must have seen early on that not only shoes, but their owners, too, might sometimes seem a little tight. And so he began a one-man anti-alcohol campaign and covered his entire establishment with various series of posters promoting sobriety. I still remember one of them. It consisted of several wordless images—they were meant to speak for themselves. My shoemaker soon realized, though, that this wouldn't do and furnished all his characters with balloons. So the father leaving the house says, "Good-bye, wife. I'm going to work." To which she replies, "I'll be waiting with dinner," while the children add in unison, "Bye bye, daddy dear!" Next picture: our hero meets a friend, "Greetings, old army pal!" "Long time no see!" "I'll drink to that!" The air is thick with balloons in the drinking scene: "Up the ladder!" "And down the hatch!" "Here's mud in your eye!" "Waiter, another round!" "Bottoms up!" Tragedy strikes in the next picture: the man stumbles out of the bar straight under an oncoming tram. Here the shoemaker knew he could get by without balloons. Then finally the epilogue. The father of the family stands on crutches in the doorway, minus one leg. The children cry, the wife wrings her hands, and a balloon streams from her lips, "There'll always be something missing from now on." And so, many years have passed, but I still remember that shoemaker and his spontaneous creations. He's doubtless long since gone to his well-earned heavenly rewards. I just worry that the inactivity may bother him. He's surrounded, after all, by winged (hence shoeless) teetotallers.

Comics by Jerzy Szylak, Wydawnictwo Znak, 2000.

Ten Minutes of Solitude

∿

THIS BOOK IS THE fruit of several years of sociological research into the emotional life of workers, especially those
who regularly deal with outside people: customers, clients,
passengers, and so on. It came out in the West, and thus describes specific conditions there, but similar situations are
starting to turn up here as well. After reading it, I came to the
paradoxical conclusion that some workers had it much easier
in the Polish People's Republic. They didn't have to pretend.
They didn't have to be polite if they didn't feel like it. They
didn't have to suppress their exhaustion, boredom, irritation.
They didn't have to conceal their lack of interest in other
people's problems. They didn't have to pretend that their
back wasn't killing them when their back was in fact killing
them. If they worked in a store, they didn't have to try to get
their customers to buy things, since the products always vanished before the lines did.

What's more, a smiling worker was no more highly valued
than a glum one. Employers even preferred the gloomy workers, since they seemed more responsible, whereas smiling
employees were automatically assumed to be cutting deals on

the side. To make all of this even sadder, people began getting used to this state of affairs. I remember my dismay and fright when I stopped for a few minutes before the window of some beautiful shop on my first visit to the West. I was spotted immediately by the salespeople and dragged inside. Even though they knew perfectly well that I wasn't going to buy a white fox-fur coat—just the cheapest handerkerchief at best. The author gives an even better story. When the first McDonald's opened in Moscow, the customers eyed the furiously bustling, smiling staff mistrustfully: so what are they laughing at? Us? Even if Sandi Mann's book had come out sooner, it couldn't have been published here anyway. Not because the censor would have spotted some perfidiously hidden praise of capitalism, since the book contains absolutely nothing of the kind. The publishers would have hesitated, since who'd be interested in such an exotic object of study: an individual capable not only of working, but of concealing his private moods. Naturally such constant camouflage must cause various kinds of stress, and stress in turn demands some sort of release. This isn't easy. The author stakes out a broad field of observation, but her advice is confined to a narrow margin. A few deep breaths. Temporary rotations in work stations. Time to blow off steam in the backroom. She gives the least space, a single sentence, to what is perhaps the best medicine: a little time spent in total solitude. She suggests ten minutes. Isn't that on the short side? And while I'm on the subject: solitude is a very good thing and every person living in an urban environment requires it sometimes. Whereas loneliness is a bad thing. When will we finally start seeing the difference between them?

Hiding What We Feel, Faking What We Don't: Understanding the Role of Your Emotions at Work by Sandi Mann, translated from the English by Hanna Wrzosek, Wydawnictwo Amber, 1999.

A Bad Little Boy

∾

Hitchcock must have been every dietician's nightmare. He lived to a ripe old age in spite of toting around perhaps a hundred pounds of excess weight his entire life. He consumed enormous quantities of fatty meats, heavy sauces, and sweets. Alcohol was his constant companion from sun-up to deepest night. As if this weren't enough, he lived in constant stress. He did battle with producers, screenwriters, and actors alike. He was a walking example of how not to live if you want to stay healthy and productive. But he just kept on working and working; few filmmakers could match him. He made fifty-three feature films, of which several have gone down in film history. More than this, they still take the viewer's breath away today. We should add to this his numerous TV shows, not to mention the films that never got made even though he spent months working on them. He did die in the end, but, if memory serves me, the same fate also awaits those who take care of themselves. You can't write a thin book about this kind of phenomenon, so Donald Spoto wrote a thick one. Hitchcock's work on every film is described and analyzed in detail. We also read different critics' opinions and

the recollections of people who knew him and had to tolerate, with humor or horror, his various whims. Finally we get
some of the master's own pronouncements. I would have
liked even more of these, since they're the book's most excit-
ing moments. His auditors were never able to pin Hitchcock
down in a sincere, confiding mood; he always got the jump
on them somehow. They were never sure when he was talking
seriously and when he was joking. And that's how Spoto
should have left him in the biography. Instead, though, the
author tries to crack him, to see what was really hiding inside
this hard nut. What were the phobias, sufferings, inhibitions,
complexes? And of course he finds all of them, but, well, what
does this add up to? It's well known, for example, that an un-
controlled appetite is frequently a reaction to failures in one's
love life. It's also well known that the world has always been
full of gluttons unhappily in love with beautiful blondes.
So why did only one of them make *Rear Window* and *The
Birds*? The mystery of talent remains a mystery. Regardless of
how many lobsters eaten in despair went into the making of
each film...But let's get back to Hitchcock and his work. On
the one hand, he was lucky, since he was recognized early on
in film circles as a master of his craft. On the other hand, he
was rarely and grudgingly viewed as an artist. Only the enthusiastic responses of European filmmakers finally earned him
that title. His movies were occasionally nominated for an
Oscar, but never won it. "Always a bridesmaid, never a bride,"
he joked graciously, although it must have smarted. I can't resist quoting a few more things. He made up his own epitaph:
"This is what happens to bad little boys." As far as I know life
and cemetery *savoir-vivre*, this project was never realized. Or
at the end of a speech before a very elegant décolletaged and
tuxedoed audience: "I'm told that a murder takes place every

minute, so I don't want to waste your precious time. I know you'd like to get back to work. Thank you."

The Dark Side of Genius: The Life of Alfred Hitchcock by Donald Spoto, translated from the English by J. S. Zaus, Wydawnictwo Alfa, 2000.

At Last

❧

I'VE HAD IT WITH those Romans," some lady doubtless cried, the lady who decided which books should be published. As a vigilant individual she was absolutely right. In a regime that proclaimed that it would endure for all time, historical research was by definition suspect. It demonstrates, after all, that nothing lasts forever—even Rome, that great empire. Some readers might derive a private, reactionary satisfaction from its fall....I don't actually know if such a lady served in this capacity at that time and if she is really the one to whom we are indebted for the appearance of Gibbon's monumental work *The Decline and Fall of the Roman Empire* in only two volumes in 1960, under the relatively benign title *Decline,* while the third volume, which dealt with the final *Fall,* failed to see the light of day. One way or another, the cry cited above illustrates well a certain reality. And now finally, forty years later, we can get our hands on the *Fall.* For those who possess the two earlier volumes this will be a great joy. But how many of them are still around? And two generations have, moreover, grown up in the meantime. So it's too bad that they didn't put out the two earlier volumes at the same time. My guess is that they lacked the funds. But they could at least have added an introduction to the third, describing the author and his work's significance for European thought. The Englishman Edward Gibbon was one of the Enlightenment's most penetrating minds. Unlike his French colleagues, though, he held conservative convictions and saw the worst possible surprises in every change. He wrote his work on Rome's fate in a state of near-despair. He saw the two-hundred-year reign of the Antonines as the empire's finest period. This was indeed a period of relative peace and cultural development. Conquered peoples (whose conquest, we should add, was always ruthless and bloody) could at that time see Rome as safeguarding their own security and growth. Unfortunately, these conquests, begun centuries earlier, could never reach their end. Each pacified nation had its own ancient enemies behind its back. Rome inherited these enemies and had once more to pacify and incorporate them. But these newly incorporated nations were in turn being tugged from the rear by still other hostile peoples. Which meant that Rome had once again to…And so on and so on. The volume *Decline* shows the consequences of this fatal necessity. Rome no longer conquered, Rome just defended itself. Still other causes contributed to the decline, and these causes had in turn their own causes. Institutions upholding laws and customs began to crumble, military discipline grew ever weaker, the citizens fell prey to doubt and a kind of sleepy satiety. The traditional tie that the old state religion had provided snapped under the pressure of Christianity's rapid growth. Christianity could not replace the earlier tie right away—it was itself internally riven, divided into many greater and lesser communities that understood the faith's truths differently. These communities agreed on only one thing: the need to stamp out paganism once and for all, to demolish its temples, statues, paintings, mosaics. The chapter describing this dogged activity, pursued across the entire expanse of the dying empire, ranks among the book's sorriest. But what can you do? An honest historian—and Gibbon tried with all his might to be just that—seldom gets the chance to say anything nice.

The Fall of the Roman Empire by Edward Gibbon, translated from the English by Irena Szymanska, annotated by Mikolaj Szymanski, PIW, 2000.

BLOCKS AND BLOCKHEADS

の

I BOUGHT THE BOOK without expecting much aside from the illustrations—which are in fact good. But what can I say? In our pictorial age I've kept a taste for reading the texts next to the pictures. The title itself took me aback. History holds a few more tyrants than that, at least some hundred thousand. Some raged briefly; others longer. Some operated in a smaller and others in a larger territory. Some confined themselves to murdering their own family; others expanded the concept of undesirable family to entire nations, and so on. How do you pick and then "round out" to one hundred? And are criteria for selection truly possible here? The author, though, didn't ask himself such questions. Anyone who came to mind got packed into the book. There are Stalin and Hitler, but beside them stands Napoleon—isn't this overdoing it? There's no Robespierre, though. The author apparently thought that his victims were just unfortunate work-related incidents. Torquemada is here, of course, but not his successors. Beria is here, but not his predecessors. Pizarro is present, but you won't find any of the other genocidal conquerers. Maybe the author simply couldn't fit them in? In that case, though, why do we find the unfortunate Ludwig II of Bavaria, who neither was, nor aspired to be, any kind of Dracula? Or, for example, Robert Menzies, the Australian premier who fell so afoul of the opposition and its ministers that he was finally forced to resign? Pol Pot, Idi Amin, and Bokassa would weep from laughter on seeing him in their midst. But what am I doing here? I've allowed myself to be drawn into a dubious game. Willy-nilly I'm starting to wonder how many corpses and terrorized people you have to leave behind to earn the title of tyrant—and how many more you have score to turn up in the ranks of the top competitors. As it turns out, the Spirit of the Age also grabs me by the hair and drags me toward its beloved scorecards, polls, graphs, "top tens," "top hundreds." This sort of thing is everywhere. If we're talking about sports, the stock market or economic figures, then fine. But certain fields should be shielded from the compilers of such lists. Culture, for example. From Tuesday to Wednesday we find out whose work has taken the lead, and who has fallen behind. Such data are analyzed immediately, even though we know ahead of time that the rankings may change from Wednesday to Thursday. Moreover, such varied works end up side by side that there's really no way to compare them. A few years back I saw a list revealing that, from the standpoint of copies published, Agatha Christie had surpassed the Bible, and Mao's "little red book" had, in turn, outsold Agatha Christie. This was supposed to prove something, but it didn't say what. It's the same with history. It can't be assembled from such stupid building blocks. Anyone who's purchased *The One Hundred Greatest Tyrants* would really have been better off buying the much cheaper and more useful *One Hundred Ways to Cook Potatoes.*

The One Hundred Greatest Tyrants by Andrew Langley, translated by Marek Maciolek, Wydawnictwo Podsiedlik, Raniowski and S-ka, 1996.

BUTTONS

രി

A BUTTON MUSEUM HAS been established in Lowicz. It has its own letterhead and has put out a book about buttons in literature. On hearing this news, some may roll their eyes and ask with a withering smile if that town's inhabitants don't have any bigger problems, and if small towns can't make do, moreover, with a couple of commemorative rooms or store windows displaying local handicrafts and stuffed fauna. No, they can't—or at least they shouldn't have to. Maybe this is just my luck, but whenever I'm traveling and want to drop by the local museum, it's either locked (the director has the key) or the young lady on duty informs me mid-visit that I'm the first person to turn up in four months. It's easy to understand why. All the most beautiful or historically significant exhibits have long since been shipped off to museums in big cities. What's left over doesn't draw anyone. Things would look different if small towns fostered institutions specializing in a given subject—a different one, of course, for every town. On spotting the sign for the Button Museum, the visitor would, after a moment of stupefaction, consider the idea, go in and take a look. And maybe even think that the town where he—he or his ancestors—was born might be better off with some nice museum or other. Maybe old postcards? Antique prayer books? Toys? Playing cards? Chessmen? If there also happened to be a diner next door where they didn't toss old socks into the soup, the town's fame would spread far. There's one other plus. Poland has many collectors. I'm not even counting those who collect any old thing any old way. I have in mind those fastidious collectors who have become true specialists in collecting and possess many genuine oddities. They have real trouble, though, in locating heirs for their collections. A family rarely appreciates the legacy left behind by a dotty granddad. If some large museum does actually take it, it will most likely be packed off to a basement storeroom. The best solution is tiny museums scattered across the entire country, thus greatly enlivening the landscape.

But let's get back to the buttons. Besides the brochure on buttons in literature, they should put out a history of buttons. About which I know next to nothing. Except that they didn't suddenly sprout on trees—some tribe must have thought them up and used them. This probably occurred sometime in the early Middle Ages. In any case the ancients weren't yet using buttons to fasten up. They employed various fibulae, buckles, and ties to this end. Otherwise the various fierce Boreases and Aquilos would have blown their robes open. And the white linen dresses of ancient Egypt? They were so tight that they couldn't be put on over one's head. They must have had discreet slits in the back, which were fastened up somehow. At this point, those prone to eye-rolling will want to ask me a question: don't I have bigger problems than the troubles of tailors on the Nile? Of course I have bigger problems. But that's no reason not to have small ones.

The Button in Literature by Zbigniew Kostrzewa, Wydawnictwo Muzeum Guzikow, 2000.

In Praise of Questions

ℐℐ

IT'S TOO BAD THAT I didn't start counting how often the word "why" comes up in this book when I began reading it. Probably several hundred times. This large number stems from one central question: What caused the great differences between various civilizations, differences that have yet to be erased? Humanity got off, after all, to pretty much the same start—little groups of hunters and gatherers scoured the Earth in search of food and shelter. So why did some remain locked in this way of life for long millennia while others managed to alter it radically? Racists (even those who would never openly admit it) have a ready answer: There are simply more and less gifted peoples. It only takes a moment's thought to see the stupidity of this answer. Intelligence isn't the issue. Archimedeses have been born everywhere, but not all of them possessed a bathtub from which to leap shrieking "Eureka!" Polar populations couldn't develop the technology for cultivating rice. Populations submerged in subtropical forests couldn't domesticate wild sheep. And you can't fault the

Aborigines for not figuring out how to milk kangaroos or at least ride them bareback. There were many such restrictions and each had its own specific consequences. To describe them the author calls upon both his own knowledge and the knowledge of others—beginning with glaciologists and ending with the historians of colonial conquests. Questions and answers, and after those answers new questions.... There's no end to it. But is that so bad? Let's do a little speculating, let's imagine some horrifically distant future in which humanity—if it's survived—will finally know everything. All questions will dry up, since there'll be no reason for them. No mysteries, hypotheses, doubts, even down to the smallest detail... Everything, including outer space investigated, checked, measured, calculated and fed into some galactic computer... The past made manifest, the present served up on a platter. And the future? Is a future still possible under such conditions? Omniscience strikes me as an incomparable disaster, paralysis of the imagination, universal silence. Since what is there to talk about if everyone knows the same things and for certain? It's a relief to know that this time will probably never come.... The book has more than five hundred pages, and its author ends with the sense that many questions connected with its main subject have yet to be explored. So much the better. I recommend this thick volume for summer vacations. I have no idea who dreamed up the idiotic notion that summer vacations require "light" reading. Just the opposite, since the "light" books get read—if any reading's done at all—before bedtime, after the office work and house work, when we lack the concentration required for heavier fare. I'll add yet another incentive, a detail that's immaterial, but pleasant. In the introduction the author mentions his wife, Marysia. So if we Poles ever meet him somewhere out there in the wide world, he's sure to understand us when we say, *"Dzien dobry."*

Guns, Germs and Steel: The Fates of Human Societies by Jared Diamond, translated from the English by Marek Konarzewski, Wydawnictwo Proszynski and Sk-a, 2000.

THE CARDBOARD-EATING CADAVER

⤕

IN COLLOQUIAL POLISH, "mollusc" means a spineless person. True molluscs should take humanity to court for defamation of character. In reality this is an ancient family, firmly grounded in its biological raisons d'être, steadfast and stalwart. It's been featured in the terrifying yet enthralling series known as evolution for some five hundred million years now. During that time it's been decimated by countless catastrophes, but it couldn't be kept down for good. Professor Andrzej Falniowski, book in hand, could be an expert witness at the trial. Since this probably won't make it to court, let's take a look at the book itself, which the author discreetly calls an outline. Some outline: 370 letter-sized pages, a twenty-three-page bibliography in tiny print, and an index of Latin names stretching in two columns over eleven pages. I won't pretend to have read it all with due attention. I've focused on molluscs and snails for the time being. Every species has its own peculiarities. For example, Botticelli's Venus is standing on a scallop. The painter didn't exaggerate; shellfish can get even bigger. At the same time there are scallop species that don't exceed a single millimeter. Or take the question of stamina. A certain snail brought from Algeria spent four years as a dead exhibit in a London museum. When some water was splashed on it by mistake, it came back to life on the spot and began consuming the cardboard on which it had been placed. Or take the matter of sexual ingenuity. When the females have no suitors in the vicinity (these hurry very slowly even when they're so inclined), they impregnate one another on their own. One such female boardinghouse was observed for twenty years, during which time ninety-three successive generations were produced. Finally the observation was terminated— from boredom, the author adds. There aren't many species of molluscs and snails in Poland. The wrong climate on land, the wrong conditions at sea. No flamboyant shapes or colors. But these yeomen showed their stuff. As soon as the glacier retreated—which had had enough time to finish off their ancient cousins—they quickly conquered the abandoned territory. They flew in, for example, on bird wings or wind-borne leaves. My favorite is the common Roman snail. This species, though, has a suicidal tendency to crawl across highways. I remember one daredevil in particular, since it had two larch needles stuck to its shell. It made it to the other side of the highway, which took it all day, from dawn to dusk. Fortunately, the highway wasn't busy that day and somehow it got there in one piece. But the next day what do I see? My Roman snail is creeping back again. To exactly the same place it started from yesterday. By now I was getting worried, so I carried it to the grass. I couldn't be sure, though, that at that moment it acknowledged the end of its reconnaissance and forsook the lethal asphalt. I stayed in that area a few days longer, but I gave a wide berth to that stretch of the road. As my aunt Kazia once told me, you've got to spare your nerves.

Steps and Missteps in the Evolution of Molluscs by Andrzej Falniowski, Wydawnictwo Polska Akademia Umiejetnosci, 2001.

NERVOUSNESS

✵

CZESLAW MILOSZ'S POETRY IN *Nonrequired Reading?* This is required reading, after all, for anyone in the habit of thinking now and then—or at least it should be. So I won't talk about his poetry here. I have a much worse idea: I'll write about myself, or, rather, about how nervous I get in the presence of both the work and its author. This started early on, in February of 1945. I'd gone to the Stary Theater in Krakow, where the first poetry reading organized since the war was about to take place. The names of the participants meant nothing to me. I was reasonably well-read in prose, but my knowledge of poetry equaled zero. Still I listened and looked. Not everyone read well. Some were unbearably bombastic, whereas others' voices broke and the paper trembled in their hands. At a certain moment they announced someone named Milosz. He read calmly, without histrionics. As if he were simply thinking out loud and inviting us to join him. "There you go," I told myself, "that's real poetry, there's a real poet." I was certainly being unfair. There were two or three other poets present who merited special attention. But exceptionality comes in degrees. My instincts told me to keep a close eye on Milosz. Not long afterward my admiration was put to a harsh test. For the first time in my life I found myself in a real restaurant on some special occasion or another. I looked around and what did I see but Czeslaw Milosz sitting nearby with friends and devouring a pork chop with sauerkraut. It was a blow. I knew in principle that even poets eat from time to time, but did they have to pick such vulgar dishes? I dealt with my horror somehow. I had more important experiences, moreover, and became a serious reader of poetry. Milosz's volume *Rescue* appeared, and I'd find new poems in the papers. My nervousness grew, became more deeply rooted with every piece I read. The next time I saw Milosz was in Paris in the late 1950s. He was wending his way through the café tables, probably meeting someone. I had the chance to go up and tell him something he might have been happy to hear— that his forbidden books were still read in Poland, transcribed in single copies that were smuggled into the country. And that anyone who tried hard enough got hold of them sooner or later. But I didn't go up and tell him. I was paralyzed by nerves. Milosz was able to return to Poland only many years later. On Krupnicza Street in Krakow the smoke of photographers with flashes and microphones almost hid him from view while crowds of us stood waiting. When he finally tore himself, exhausted, from the reporters, the autograph hunters surrounded him in turn. I lacked the courage to pester him in that mob, to introduce myself and maybe ask for an autograph. I had the pleasure of meeting him personally only during his second visit to Poland. Many things have changed since that time, but in one sense nothing's different. Admittedly, I've found many opportunities to talk with him, to meet him in the company of mutual friends, even to read together at various affairs and suffer together at official functions. But to this day I still have no idea how to deal with such a Great Poet. I'm as nervous around him as I ever was. Even though we sometimes crack jokes and clink glasses of well-chilled vodka. And even though once in a restaurant we both happened to order the same pork chops with sauerkraut.

From Szymborska's column "Nonrequired Reading" in the newspaper *Gazeta Wyborcza*, Saturday–Sunday, June 30–July 1, 2001, page 9. Special supplement in honor of Czeslaw Milosz's ninetieth birthday.

TRANSLATOR'S NOTE

𝒥𝒫

I WANT TO THANK my great friend and sometime collaborator, Stanislaw Baranczak, Szymborska's First Secretary extraordinaire, Michal Rusinek, and my wonderful editor Drenka Willen for all kinds of help beyond the call of duty. I'd also like to thank my family, Michael and Martin Lopez, for enthusiastic assistance on everything from gladiators to continental drift.

I selected the sketches in this volume from the three volumes of *Non-Required Reading* (*Lektury nadobowiazkowe*) Szymborska has published in book form and from recent, uncollected sketches that Szymborska very kindly passed on to me as I was working on this project.

CPSIA information can be obtained at www.ICGtesting.com
Printed in the USA
LVOW042136220712

291111LV00001B/29/A